The Nature of Things

Twenty-four stories about embracing reality

Brigid Elsken Galloway

Flamepoint, Inc.
Birmingham, Alabama

THE NATURE OF THINGS:

Twenty-four stories about embracing reality

Copyright © 2016 Brigid Elsken Galloway

All rights reserved. No part of this book may be used or reproduced by any means without the written permission of the author, except in the case of brief, attributed quotations embodied in critical articles and reviews.

ISBN 13: 978-1537152660

Library of Congress Control Number: 2016914577

Published by Flamepoint, Inc., Birmingham, Alabama

Printed in the United States of America

Photo of the author by Vincent Remini

For Jack, who woke me up.

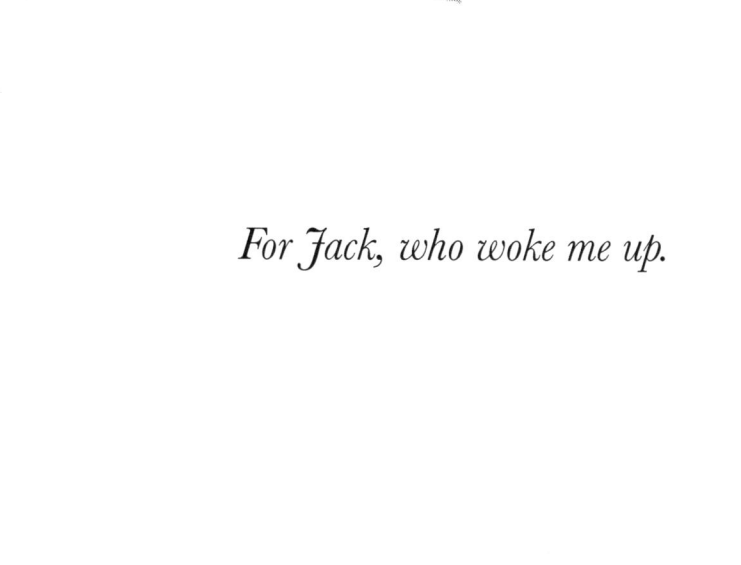

ACKNOWLEDGMENTS

This book would not be possible without every person and experience I have been given throughout my life. I am so very grateful for all the circumstances — positive and negative, joyous and tragic — that have brought me to this place of understanding.

Among my greatest teachers are my parents, Greg and Catherine Elsken; my sisters, Gretchen, Mary and Katrina, who were always there for me; my wonderful circle of friends, who encouraged me along the way; and my son Jack, who makes me laugh, challenges me to keep learning, and reminds me to remain present.

Thank you to my spiritual mentors: Muriel Thompson, Joe and Lark Howell; and my fellow faculty members at The Institute for Conscious Being who took me in and nourished my soul; and to all my 12-Step friends who guide me and provide perspective.

And to my love Jason Haessly, I am so grateful for your presence in my life, and for traveling this path with me.

Contents

Introduction

Nowhere to Run ix

Chapter 1: Awareness

The Not-So-Happy Meal 1

Into the Unknown 16

Chapter 2: Acceptance

The Take-Back Queen 23

The Worst Best Day 30

Chapter 3: Surrender

Life After Waffles 43

Hello, Crisis Hotline 53

Chapter 4: Honesty

Leaving Eden 67

Selfie 74

Chapter 5: Compassion

Tiny Seed. Big Lesson. 79

Attack of the Killer Be's 86

Chapter 6: Presence

Obedience School 93

God's Minute 98

Contents

Chapter 7: Humility

Scars 109

Growing Up 117

Chapter 8: Reconciliation

Lighting Up..........................125

Dust to Dust 132

Chapter 9: Forgiveness

Christmas Past, Present, Perfect.........139

Auld Lang Syne...................150

Chapter 10: Healing

Away Camp..........................157

Salvation...............................163

Chapter 11: Consciousness

Occupied China...................169

The Nature of Things 173

Chapter 12: Practice

Un-Stuck 177

Birds of the Air....................182

Introduction

Nowhere to Run

When I was eight years old I became angry with my mother. I vowed to run away from home. At this ripe, young age, I had already experienced enough dissatisfaction and inequity to long for freedom. Imagine that. I cannot even recall what heinous demand my mother made upon me. Perhaps she insisted I tidy my room, or do my homework before watching *The Brady Bunch*, or take a bath. Whatever it was, that injustice instilled in me a distinct romantic desire to leave and make my own way in the world. Of course, this was impossible to do for an eight-year-old in 1970. To make matters worse, we lived on a small farm in a rural area just outside of Little Rock, Arkansas. Even if I were to run away, there was really nowhere for me to run.

In my moment of indignation, I wanted to storm out of my parents' house and never return, but there was just one problem: I had school the next day. I wasn't so terribly angry with my mother that I would dare miss seeing my beloved fourth grade teacher. So I filed away my grievance and decided that over the weekend I would make a break for it.

On Saturday morning, after eating a bowl of Rice Krispies and watching *The Scooby Doo Mystery Hour*, I packed up a few of my prized possessions in my Snoopy backpack and left home.

It was late March and the morning air was still and crisp and clean. Dew lay heavy on the overgrown lawn. My Dad wasn't much on yard work. He pressed into service a few living lawn mowers (otherwise known as Jersey heifers) to chomp down the weeds. Of course, the law mowers left dark piles of dung on the ground, and I learned early on to carefully pick my way when I went out to play.

As I surveyed the possibilities for my new residence, my white cat, Molly, rubbed against my legs. The sun was already warm and I felt an urgency to go, although I had nothing to do, nowhere to be, no one to conspire with, except my cat. This day was the first I longed for something more in my life, although I could not yet imagine what that something was.

Not wanting to be discovered by my family, I ran through the damp grass to the hay barn where I set up my new home. Molly followed me and promptly lay down in a sunspot. I set down my backpack, but was not so contented. What would I do all day by myself?

From my pack, I retrieved several strips of crisp bacon that I squirreled away from breakfast. My cat sniffed the air but didn't leave her spot. I quickly consumed the salty pork, grateful that I brought along a thermos of instant Nestea. I took a sip from the tinny-tasting thermos and felt the half-dry, undissolved globs of tea melt into bitterness in my mouth. The saccharin sweetener served no antidote. I kicked at a hay bale. I was already bored.

When would my mother begin to miss me? Would she be sorry for the way she treated me? Would she regret that she had been so cruel? I imagined her panic when she realized that I had made good my threat. I checked my little Timex watch and discovered that it was only 10:15 a.m. I had only been "missing" for about 30 minutes. Now what?

I unpacked the contents of my backpack: a *Trixie Belden* mystery, my favorite stuffed animal, Miss Kitty, and my glow-in-the-dark statue of the boy Jesus. He was posed with his arms extended as he taught in the temple right before his distraught parents found him and chewed him out for worrying them so.

I also brought my little red beaded change purse. It held all of 17-cents. I suppose it didn't occur to me that I should pack a change of clothes or a blanket or take more money. I didn't have much foresight or experience as a runaway. The 17-cents had promise though as I thought about the little convenience store down the road and their candy display. I grabbed up my backpack, left Molly behind and set out walking to Rainey's Market feeling very independent and grown up.

The little market was a mile away and on the other side of the busy highway, which my parents absolutely forbade me to cross. But that was no problem for a fugitive, like me. I boldly walked into the store and made my purchase: 17-cents worth of Tootsie rolls, Ice Cubes, Sixlets and Now & Laters. Grasping the brown paper bag full of penny candy, I crossed the street again and began the return trip.

Of course, there were no sidewalks out in the country. I walked in the ditches among the tall weeds and cattails. At one point, I stepped into a marsh, soaking my sneakers and socks. The cars sped past like angry wasps, and I began to wish I had stayed in the hay barn.

About a block or so away from my house, I began to feel cool relief. I was almost home when a familiar red Chevy pickup passed me. I glanced up in time to meet my father's eyes. Adrenalin shot through my body as I realized what I had done. I sprinted the rest of the way home, hoping beyond hope that Daddy hadn't really seen me stomping through the tall weeds so close to the highway.

Of course, he had. The look of disappointment on my father's face delivered far more punishment than words could express. I burst into tears and sobbed my apologies. Tears could always melt my father's stern veneer. Was I sorry that I had disobeyed my parents' rules? Or was I just upset that I had been caught? Indeed, I was thrilled with my little adventure. I had walked a mile up the road to the store and back again without a mishap. I had crossed the terrible highway without being hurt. I began to question. Did my parents want to protect me, or were they trying to keep me from exploring the world on my own?

Although I did not run away from home again, on that day I left Eden never to return. This became the first of my many departures.

Much in the same way, at age 47, I didn't mean to embark on a spiritual journey. Really. I assure you, I didn't. Like the eight-year-old me, I thought I was just going to the convenience store for some candy, but here I am, quoting Buddha and Jesus and finding meaning in everything from Alzheimer's disease to Happy Meals.

Some days it feels bizarre, but the alternative is to remain in a state of anger and confusion.

What does it mean to realize one's spiritual journey? Sometimes it's easy to think this path has been laid out for me and I merely have to pick up the breadcrumbs. In my Catholic life, this is what I believed. I thought God had a grand plan for all the world (including me), and as long as I kept his commandments and believed in Jesus as my Savior, I would wind up at the end of the rainbow, otherwise known as Heaven.

When my A+ life turned to a D- (death, divorce, disease, downsizing), it was hard to reconcile how a compassionate God allowed these "bad things" to happen. It was easier to throw in the towel and just sit down and shout, "There is no path!" or to think God was a sadistic jerk.

I began to feel that I deserved the D's, and that I was being punished because I thumbed my nose at religion along the way. After all, for a very long time, I thought I was too smart for God. Maybe God had gone *Old Testament* on me, casting me out to wail and gnash my teeth?

Not long after I hit my emotional and spiritual wall, I began seeing Muriel the Friendly Therapist and she handed me a copy of Pema Chodron's *When Things Fall Apart*. I attribute that book to being the first of many insightful texts that have helped end my teeth gnashing.

Chodron is an American Buddhist nun who credits her intense hatred of her husband as the reason she began practicing Buddhism. "The spiritual journey is not about heaven and finally getting to a place that's really swell," she writes. "In fact, that way of looking at things is what keeps us miserable ... The spiritual journey involves going beyond hope and fear, stepping into unknown territory, continually moving forward."[1]

During this formative year on my spiritual path, Buddhist meditation and mindfulness practices helped me become aware of the true nature of my life's dissatisfaction. As I began to observe my unhealthy emotions — anger, frustration, envy, stinginess, fear, regret, resentment, shame and guilt — I saw patterns that formed in their wake. Although my mother (or my editor, or my ex-husband) might trigger strong feelings of anger, disappointment or fear, it was not that person, per se, who was the source of my unhappiness. Because if that person were to blame, then now that I was no longer married, no longer gainfully employed and no longer caring for my dying parents, I should be fine, right? Yet, this was not the case. In fact, I struggled more. At least now — thanks to my heightened sense of awareness — I saw I was stuck, and this knowledge allowed a teeny, tiny light of perspective to pierce my otherwise foggy, stuck way of thinking. I realized I needed other tools to help me overcome my habitual responses. That's when I did the thing that I never, ever thought I would do: I joined a 12-Step group.

I knew next to nothing about 12-Step recovery before I went through my big, fat, emotional meltdown. How does a college-educated journalist get to be almost 50 years old and not know more than what she's seen on a few sit-coms about one of the most effective inter-spiritual organizations on the planet?

Like most people, I thought 12-Step recovery was for loser drug addicts, prescription junkies and drunks. Since I had no idea that control was an addiction, it never occurred to me that there might be a 12-Step program for people like me. When I began attending 12-Step meetings, a new world opened up to me.

At first the trite slogans and "Higher Power" talk made me uncomfortable. I had to set aside my fears, my preconceived notions and my aversion to cute sayings. I had to be willing to give the methodology behind the Steps a chance.

Today, my spiritual journey has brought me to a place where I can begin to accept reality rather than rail against it. I am beginning to see that what *is* may be far more wonderful than what I thought I wanted — and that ability to let go of my ideas about my life seems to be the key to happiness.

"Everything that occurs in our confused mind we can regard as the path," Chodron writes. "Everything is workable."[2]

When I begin to perceive life's difficulties as workable rather than insurmountable, I can go about the business of discovering the beauty in all of life — not just the pleasant parts. I am no longer stuck. My mother's death by dementia becomes workable. My humiliating second divorce becomes workable. My off-the-wall efforts to control my preteen son are workable, too — if I am willing to see what my limited perceptions are really showing me about myself.

Until I was willing to embrace the reality of my life, I could not see these truths about myself. I could finally stop beating myself up for being human and imperfect, and begin to glimpse a deeper understanding of others and myself. I could begin to develop a little thing called compassion.

Of course, my lessons aren't laid out for me with big neon directional signals pointing the way. The spiritual path is more like one of those reality cooking show competitions where you're given a box of risotto, raw cow tongue, a bag of dill-flavored potato chips and a half dozen kiwi and expected to build a gourmet meal featuring those ingredients. I have to be willing to work with what I am given. Not just the delicious, yummy stuff, but also the disgusting, revolting stuff too. In truth, the revolting stuff may be the stuff that provides the most nutritional value and growth along the path.

In hindsight, everything I went though — the loss, pain, disappointment, frustration and downright craziness — was all necessary for me to get to the place where I am today. On most days, I'm not sure that's saying a lot. I mean it's not like I'm breathing rarified air here. Most days, I'm still stumbling around in the dark. But as we say in the South, even a blind pig finds a truffle every now and then.

Chapter 1: Awareness

The Not-So-Happy Meal

Sometime after I left for college, my mother planted holly bushes and pines along the drive between the house and the highway. The city had expanded the road from two lanes to four and the natural screen was my mother's only way to shut out the view. The pines were scraggly saplings when my father plunged his post-hole digger into the earth to plant them. Mother watered them everyday and protected them from frosts. After twenty years of growth, she finally had her wish: the house was hidden.

Years ago, before the city annexed West Little Rock, our house was considered in the country. My parents' little farm — with its cows and pigs and large vegetable garden — was typical for the rural area. Once the developers came, farms and woodlands were transformed into strip malls. The landscape no longer resembled the place where I grew up.

The trees and shrubs in front of my parents' house grew so tall and dense that passersby could not see the old rock house from the road. Even after all these years, I almost drove past the familiar driveway.

The porch light cast a yellowish glow on the Nandina bushes. Although thorny vines tangled their simple branches, the Nandina did its best to look festive by setting out red berries, lovely but poisonous. The stone house itself was unchanged, yet it seemed smaller, as if its structure was shrinking with the same aging process as my parents, who were now well into their 80s.

As your parents reach this age, you hope to appreciate all the nuances about them. You want to breath them in like air. You hope to remember all those tiny details later. The sound of voice and laughter. The smell of fried chicken. The warm embrace. The coolness of their hands in yours.

I tried to cling to these sensory gifts, though almost immediately they began to fade. Sometime during each visit, patient appreciation gave way to reality, and I remembered the reason I left again and again: This home no longer contained my life.

Brass bells bound with hay bailing twine announced our arrival.

"Come in, come in," my Mother said, her soft voice breaking with the remnants of a cold.

I bent slightly to hug her. She was so thin. When had she become so thin? I placed my hand on Jack's back and prompted him to step closer. He hugged his grandmother around the legs as she bent to extend her arms around him.

"Oh, Jack, you've gotten so big!" Mom said.

The next thing I noticed was what was not there: the Christmas tree.

Every year we placed the tree in the same spot, to the left of

Dad's red chair. Some years when the tree was too crooked, my father had to fasten fishing line between the tree and a nail in the wall to anchor it in place. We never bought a tree. Dad carried his saw across the street into woods and cut a fresh tree down. Most years he chose a cedar with its imperfect, crooked trunk and sticky branches that made my arms itch. No matter their shape or size, these homegrown trees were always proclaimed perfect by the time their branches were weighed down with lights and ornaments and shiny, glass balls, and strewn with silver tinsel that shimmered and spun when the air stirred.

Not this year. Decorating a tree was too much for my mother to accomplish this year. Besides, Jack (who was almost four and very much believed in Santa), and I (who was 44 and very much believed in creating the perfect Christmas), would be back home before Christmas Eve. Yet I felt the absence of our tradition, the lack of cedar aroma and the glint of multicolored lights. It shouldn't have mattered, but somehow it did.

Mother moved slowly, balancing herself on the doorframe as she walked from the living room to the kitchen. Among her known health concerns were osteoporosis and high blood pressure. After experiencing what she first called a "mild heart attack" (and later insisted was nothing at all), her doctor placed her on a low-cholesterol, low-salt diet, which she followed dutifully. Mom had been a nurse after all. She once worked in surgery. She knew how to follow the instructions of doctors.

"Are you hungry?" Mother asked.

"No," I said, following her to the kitchen. "Jack couldn't wait this late to eat, so we stopped at Wendy's on the way."

"Oh? Well, you must still want something! I have some cookies out in the freezer. I bet Jack would like a sugar cookie! I've got some icing made up, too. Jack, do you want to icing some cookies with Grandma?"

Slice-n-bake was anathema in our home. Mom was famous for her sugar cookies. They were buttery, sweet, crisp and thin. The process of making sugar cookies from scratch was time consuming, but she always made them before every major holiday. She had dozens of cookie cutters that she had collected over the years. My favorite — and the oldest — were made of a thick red plastic and had fancy indentations that would imprint details into the dough. There were Santas, reindeer, wreaths, angels, camels (for the Three Wise Men) and snowmen; rabbits, chicks and egg shapes for Easter; shamrocks for Saint Patrick's Day; hearts at Valentines; and stars and flags for the Fourth of July. She had a menagerie of circus animals, dinosaurs and barnyard critters, too. She often took cookies to church functions when children would be present, and always had some ready for her grandchildren.

I was sent to the old garage (which to my knowledge never housed an automobile) to forage through a large, deep freezer to find the frozen cookies. It was an enormous white, metal beast that held everything from milk and cheese to steaks and potato chips. Mom hated to see food spoil.

I lifted the door of the freezer, pulling against its vacuum seal. A cloud of cold air issued forth and it took me a minute to orient myself to the items cast in frost. Mother labeled most of the packages with slips of paper attached by a rubber band. There were also plastic containers of chicken broth, egg yolks, breadcrumbs, fresh parsley and lemon juice. No item was too minuscule to save for future use. A child of the Depression, Mom's sense of practical frugality hadn't waned over the decades.

As promised, the jar of sugar cookies was in the back left corner of the freezer, behind the saltine crackers. A film of condensation covered the container as I carried it into the warm house. Jack was sitting on his knees on a chair at the kitchen table, a dishtowel tied around his waste as an apron. Mom held a small bowl in which she was showing him how to mix red food coloring into white icing. She stirred with a toothpick until the sweet stuff was a bright pink. Then she picked up another bowl, dabbed a bit of white icing in it and added blue food color.

"To make Santa's eyes," she explained. "The eyes really make him come alive."

On she went, creating green and yellow and a dab of orange. Meanwhile, the fog on the jar of frozen cookies began to disperse and I could discern an unusual yellow cast to the contents.

I opened the jar and removed a few cookies. Usually, crisp and clearly defined, this batch was thick, hard and misshaped. Had she added too much baking powder? Or used self-rising flour? Something was distinctly off. The cookies possessed a faint sulfur, eggy odor, perhaps the reason for their yellow hue. Mom didn't seem to notice, nor did Jack, who grabbed a cookie and nibbled at its frozen edges. Mother picked up a cookie shaped somewhat like a Christmas stocking and began to apply a thick layer of green icing.

In most aspects of life — with money, sex, religion, politics — Mother was conservative, but when it came to decorating her sugar cookies, she was downright decadent. She spent hours carefully glazing each cookie with buttery-sweet icing, adding red hots for Santa's nose and coconut beards. The reindeer got red noses, too. Camels received special attention, often sporting silver dragees on their ornately iced backs. They were modeled after a picture Mom clipped from a magazine.

Tonight the icing clumped in little pockets where the powder sugar had not integrated into the butter and milk and it formed an acne of tiny sugar lumps. Mother placed the stocking down on a tray on the table, and picked up a camel.

I tried not to stare as she labored through the process of applying the thick icing. By this time, Jack abandoned his cookie to play in the adjoining room with all the old familiar toys that Grandma kept for his visits.

"Oh fiddle!" Mom said. "I just can't get this eye right."

I looked at the camel. Instead of a delicate dot of icing for an eye, he had a big glob of blue across his nose.

"Let me help," I said, taking the cookie from her.

I did my best to transform the blue glob into a bridle and reigns and then applied the slightest dab of icing to make an eye. It looked better, but not like Mom's famous designs.

Sitting down at the table across from her, I watched her cover an angel in white icing, her slender fingers grasping the knife. Then she handed the cookie to me to place the small details. Blue eyes, yellow halo, an oval mouth of pink. We worked together like this for a while.

I didn't know that this odd batch of Christmas cookies would be her last. The slow unraveling of her mind was gradual and subtle, her thoughts catching on the sticky edges of the past.

Almost a year later, when Dad suffered a heart attack and was moved to a hospice facility, Mom insisted on staying with him. My sisters and I knew she could not return to their old house alone. The hospice had a little daybed and she moved into the room with my Dad. The shock of almost losing the man she'd been married to for more than 50 years was almost more than she could handle.

Despite his diagnosis, Dad improved, but Mom continued to spiral into the stages of dementia. That spring my sisters and I moved our parents into Pleasant Hills, an aptly named retirement community. Her condition worsened. She refused to eat, hid her pills and hallucinated.

I knew she was sick, but I just wanted her to be my Mom again. I bought her B12 and tried to ply her appetite with ice cream and fried chicken. Yet, nothing I could do or say would change her condition or her ability to relate to the world in the way I needed her to relate to it. Finally, my sisters and I took Mom to a geriatric specialist who diagnosed her with vascular dementia. Although we could help manage her symptoms (insomnia, depression, lack of appetite, high blood pressure) through medication, her disease was unmanageable, and my life had become unmanageable, too.

The following summer, I had recently taken a new job, but I made the six-hour drive to Little Rock to visit my parents. I don't recall the exact reason for this particular trip. Perhaps it was to celebrate a birthday, or simply because my schedule allowed it. Maybe Mom had a doctor's appointment. Thinking back now, I'm sure there was no immediate medical trauma, because I brought

Jack with me. It was the first of many "last times to see Grandma and Grandpa" trips we would make.

Mother was in what I would later understand as Stage Five of degenerative dementia. She was still able to walk (with assistance) and communicate, although not clearly, but her perception of reality had shifted. In some ways, this stage was the most difficult because she was still present as the mother we knew and loved, but her appearance and demeanor had changed drastically. We begged her to use her walker, to eat more, to take her medication. She still knew our names, but stumbled over simple words and became frustrated by the fog in her brain.

To Jack, she was just Grandma. He knew she was sick, but he (thankfully) didn't comprehend the gravity of her illness. Jack loved visiting Pleasant Hills with its maze of hallways and frequent elevators. He could help himself to ice cream in the dining room, and there was always candy in a bowl in the lobby. The residents doted on him, as they did on all children who visited. Jack thought Pleasant Hills was a swanky hotel.

For me, the trip was arduous. I wanted to spend time with my parents, but once there, I was overcome with their frailty and all that came with it. Their apartment was too hot and stuffy for midsummer in the South. Although it had two bedrooms, the scant 600-square-foot layout was too small to spend extended periods of time with a 5-year-old. My mother's caregiver hovered, which was both wonderful and frustrating. There was nowhere to run or hide from the oppressive sense of the inevitable.

Jack didn't notice the clutter or chaos that I saw. His toy-seeking radar took him straight to the cupboard, where he retrieved a tattered, red box. Inside were Grandpa's old dominos — a well-worn set of ivory double-nines turned cheddar-cheese yellow. Jack was thrilled with this discovery and dumped them from the box. Over the years, my Dad and I played dominos together. The game was a great equalizer. No matter my demeanor or age, I could relate to my Dad in multiples of five.

The cool tiles clattering out on the tabletop calmed my nerves for a while as I sat with my Dad and Jack and focused on the game. We slowly explained the rules to Jack, who caught on quickly, and then pouted when he lost. Grandpa took pity and threw the next game to him — something he never did for his daughters. To us, he showed no mercy when it came to sending us to the "bone yard" for more tiles.

Mother tottered in and out of the room worrying over things she could no longer remember. She wanted to return to their old house and retrieve some items, or to live there again. Either option was impossible. It had been eight months since they lived there and the home was in a hopeless state of disrepair. But it was futile to explain to her why she couldn't return there. Thankfully, Mom's caregiver distracted her with a promise to take her to church on Sunday.

We could not have survived without a Mom's caregiver. She was patient when I was not. She filled the apartment with prattle as she went about her tasks, helping mother to bath and dress and eat.

When Jack became frustrated with dominos, and I with the heat and noise, we went for a walk around the grounds of Pleasant Hills. There wasn't a playground, of course, but there was a bench swing surrounded by plastic flowers in a perpetual garden.

When we returned to the apartment, Dad was reading the newspaper as Mom napped in the next room. Mom's caregiver recounted my Mom's bowel movements and every item she consumed for lunch. Jack busied himself with a puzzle from the cupboard and then began to complain he was hungry. I felt guilty for leaving, and worse for staying. There was no easy answer to be found.

On our drive back to my sister's house, I stopped at McDonald's to pick up dinner for Jack. Idling beside the drive-thru kiosk, Jack spotted the Happy Meal®. The new *Pirates of the Caribbean* movie had just been released and there was a particularly cute Jack Sparrow doll being offered as the Happy Meal toy.

Although I hate being suckered into buying food to get a toy that Jack didn't know he wanted before he saw it, the day had beat down my resolve and I gave into his request. A Happy Meal is such a simple thing to be able to give my child. I set aside my aversion for cheap marketing ploys — which, I knew all about since I was one of those evil marketers who concocted enticing gimmicks — and ordered the Happy Meal with chicken nuggets, fries and (yes) a Coke.

Jack was thrilled. Although we often indulged in fast-food nuggets, getting the Happy Meal was special. I told him that he had been so good and patient at Grandma and Grandpa's that he deserved this treat. And the Jack Sparrow toy looked to be a better than average break-in-two-seconds-or-end-up-under-foot-on-the-floor kinda prize. I paid at the first window, and then pulled around and was handed the trademark Happy Meal box, resplendent with *Pirates* licensed imagery.

"Okay, Jack," I said. "Food first, toy later."

When I opened the box, I saw that something was distinctly, terribly wrong. On top of the piping hot French fries was a hard-plastic car with *The Incredibles* logo plastered over it. What foul trickery was this?

A white-hot fury settled over me. I said a curse word that most parents do not want to say in front of their five-year-old-parrots. The perky McDonald's worker had already shut the glass window and walked away, but I had not pulled my car forward yet.

"Excuse me!" I yelled into the closed drive-thru window.

The McDonald's worker appeared and slid open the glass.

"Can I help you?" she chirped.

"This isn't Johnny Depp," I said flatly. "My son loves Jack Sparrow. We thought we were getting the Jack Sparrow toy. Don't you have any of those left?"

"I'm sorry," the McDonald's girl said. "We ran of the *Pirates of the Caribbean* toys."

Another wave of white-hot rage came over me.

"If you are out of those toys," I said indignantly. "You should take down the sign for them! That's false advertising!"

"I'm sorry, Mam," the girl said.

The white-hot anger consumed my brain. I forgot my saner, better self. I'd been duped!

"I never buy Happy Meals because I don't believe in them," I said. "But today, I decided to treat my son because he likes Jack Sparrow. And his name is Jack! His Grandpa's name is Jack! I wouldn't have bought the damn Happy Meal if I'd known I'd get a stupid *Incredibles* toy!"

"I'm sor—," the girl began.

"When did that *Incredibles* movie come out, anyway? 2006!" I shouted. "That was last summer!"

The girl was maybe 20 years old. I could have been her mother. She stared blankly at me. She placed her hand on the sliding glass window, ready to end my diatribe.

"I'm sorry, Mam," she said sincerely. "There's really nothing I can do."

Then from the back seat, I heard a little voice, small and soft, like the voice deep inside you that can be heard if only you're quiet enough to listen.

"Mom," Jack said, "it's okay. I like this toy. It's good."

The current of my anger broke. I saw how hopelessly ridiculous I was acting. There was nothing I could do to right this wrong. I was promised one thing and given another: this toy, this mother, this diagnosis, this life. Nothing was what I wanted it to be.

Jack's little voice reached the last thread of my sanity. I pulled away from the drive-thru window and drove into a nearby parking space and turned off the motor. With all my might I flung the toy car onto the passenger-side floor mat, and let loose a shout. Then I placed my head on the steering wheel and began to sob.

After a few moments I raised my head and glanced at Jack's image in the rearview mirror. His eyes were large and he held the Happy Meal box in his hands as if there were a rattlesnake inside.

"I'm sorry, son," I said. "I guess Happy Meals do **not** make Mommy happy."

"I don't ever, ever want to get a Happy Meal again," Jack said earnestly.

Ugh. Just when I thought it was impossible for me to feel worse about my life and my self, I realized I'd been a complete and total bitch to that poor McDonald's girl, and my son witnessed it all. Jack didn't care about getting the wrong toy. He loved getting Happy Meals even if the toys were cheap and usually ended up in the trash by the time we arrived home. I was the one acting like a child.

Fortunately, my reaction to the *Incredibles'* car was so over the top that I was able to see what was really going on in my crazy mind. My anger had little to do with false advertising or the seductive false promise of Happy Meals. My meltdown had nothing to do with McDonald's, or toys, or Jack, for that matter. I was furious that my mother was so sick that she could hardly piece a sentence together. I was outraged that my Mom would never be the same again. She was dying and there was nothing I could do about it, and to make matters worse, she had lost her mind! She was gone. Although still living, she was gone.

Even worse, I hated what was left of her. I hated that she hid her medications and thought we were conspiring against her. I was appalled at how she picked at her food, how her hands shook and the messes she made. How could this be the same woman who meticulous stitched the lace on my wedding gown? This decrepit old woman was not my mother! My mother was gone. Her frail, thin body breathed, but this was not the woman who raised me. That woman was now ruined and wasted and gone, gone, gone.

Beneath that feeling of desperation to have something returned to me that was lost forever was another even more desperate thought: What if this happens to me? What if I develop dementia, too? It could happen. I knew the statistics. They say that if we live long enough, we will all die with Alzheimer's. The thought made me want to scream. I did not want to die like my mother, slowly losing my mind, my identity, my sense of security and appreciation for life. Her disease seemed like a form of torture. That is not life, I thought. I don't want to live that way. If I ever got like that, I'd want someone to put me out of my misery.

Of course, my mother was so sick that she was not aware of how profoundly her mind and body were failing. That's the paradox of dementia: At a certain stage, the person experiencing the phenomenon of memory loss and warped thought processes isn't aware of it. It's the family members who are still cognitively astute and aware who experience the misery.

Into this circle of hell I fell. My anger, my tears, my grief bound me up and left me powerless, without any hope of escape. I wasn't grieving my mother. I was crying for myself. I was so very lost.

At this moment, from the backseat of the car, Jack's presence brought me back to my reality.

'Mom?" Jack said. "I'm sorry I wanted a Happy Meal."

Jack. Oh, my God! Now he thinks he's done something wrong. I took a deep breath, wiped the tears from my face and turned in my seat to face him.

"Oh honey, it's not your fault," I said. "I'm sorry. I'm just so tired and I'm sad about Grandma. She's very sick, honey, and it makes me sad to see her that way."

"But she'll get better soon, right?" Jack said.

"No, honey, there's no getting better. Grandma's very old and sick. She has dementia and that means her brain isn't working right. And she's very frail and ... it's just what happens ..."

My voice trailed off. I smiled at Jack.

"It's okay, honey. Please, eat your chicken nuggets," I said.

I reached down and retrieved the *Incredibles* car and handed it to my son. As we drove back to my sister's house, I heard him making those rumbly noises that little boys create while running something — anything — with wheels across a semi-flat surface. "Vroom! Vroom!"

Even in my exhausted state, I recognized that sound, even if I couldn't feel it for myself: It was the sound of contentment. It was the feeling that all would be **OK** no matter what. Regardless of illnesses or setbacks or disappointments, it was the childlike optimism that happiness could be found in whatever was right before you. I wondered if I would ever feel that sense of contentment again.

Into the Unknown

As I neared Hospice Home, I was anxious about seeing my mother. She'd been admitted to the nursing facility earlier in the week and, according to my sisters who had been with her, she was comfortable but disoriented. Hospice is not typically a designation that you would desire for your parents, but in Mom's case, it was a blessing.

After living in a small apartment with our dad for the past year, she'd finally gotten to the point where she could not get out of bed on her own. Mom required around the clock care, but the thought of placing her in a traditional nursing home was not an attractive option. The last time she'd been hospitalized, she was released into a rehabilitation center (aka nursing home). The experience was beyond depressing, and left our Mom more disoriented than ever.

Over the months since her diagnosis with vascular dementia, we'd seen a steady and progressive decline in our mother's mental and physical health. So as strange as it might sound, Mom's move to inpatient hospice care was a relief. We begged her geriatrician for the designation. After managing her ever-changing medical needs, my sisters and I were exhausted of options and hope. We had come to accept reality.

At first we called her illness "absent-mindedness." She left her purse in the shopping cart at Kroger and forgot to turn off the gas burner beneath the kettle. Now she couldn't recall what day it was or where she was. I knew Mom was no longer fully present, but I wasn't prepared for my visit that day.

Mother lay in bed, her eyes closed, mouth agape. She had become so very frail and thin she was almost skeletal. A crime show rerun played on TV and I found the remote control and changed to The Disney Channel. I told Jack, who was five, that we had to be quiet in Grandma's room. He took a seat on the daybed by the window and began playing a Pokémon game on his Nintendo DSi. I kissed my mother's forehead.

"Mom," I said softly, "it's Brigid and Jack. We've come from Birmingham for a visit."

Mother stirred, opened her eyes slightly and then closed them again. The phrase "playing 'possum" came to my mind. Was she pretending to sleep?

I sat down on the side of the bed and took her cool hand in mine. I chattered about our drive from Birmingham to Little Rock and how Jack had been good on the seven-hour trip. I told her that we were staying with my sister and that I when I came back for another visit in the morning I'd bring Dad with me.

Did my idle chitchat bore her, or she really was sleeping? Either way, the sweet reunion I'd imagined did not take place. The odors of air freshener and urine and cafeteria meatloaf mingled together in the confines of the room. The shades were up and I could see the sun was starting to set. A firefly flashed on the lawn.

"Jack, want to catch lightning bugs outside?" I asked.

Hospice Home was designed with visiting families in mind. Every room had a door to the outside, an egress for escape in case of a fire, but it came in handy for family members who needed a breath of fresh air or a cigarette. I had stopped before we arrived at Hospice Home, leaving Jack occupied with his video game while I stood behind the car puffing away, pretending to find something in the trunk that did not exist. I could not smoke now, not with Jack and not in such proximity to my mother, but the distraction of walking outside into the warm night air helped calm me.

Jack and I slipped outside and raced across the grass to the young oak trees at the edge of the property. He chased after lightning bugs that seemed to disappear just as he was about to grasp them. We played tag and looked for tadpoles in the little stream that bordered the property. When the sun obliged us with pink and gold streaks across the darkening sky, we went back to my mother's room. We found her sitting up in bed, an aide feeding her dinner. Mom looked in our direction but did not acknowledge us. I introduced myself to the nurse's aide.

"Your daughter and grandson are here!" she said loudly.

My mother nodded. I walked near the bed, positioning Jack directly in front of me so she could see him since her eyesight was limited.

"Hi Mom," I said. "How are you doing?"

Mom stared at the spoon as the aid prompted her with another bite of applesauce. Jack fidgeted away from my grasp and climbed back into the window seat. I watched the aid deliver spoonfuls of mashed potatoes and bites of meatloaf to my invalid mother.

Mom didn't like meatloaf. She never made it for us when we were growing up. I felt an aversion rise up in me as I watched her spit out a piece of meat. The aide softly scolded her and slipped the bite back in my mother's mouth as though she was an infant.

I knew I should say something gracious, like, "Oh, let me do that!" But I didn't want to feed my mother. I didn't want to change her Depends or give her a sponge bath. I hated myself for not being the type of daughter who brings her infirm parents into her home to nurse them. I wanted to justify myself by saying children are not supposed to do these tasks for their mothers, but, then, I was no longer a child. I was 45 years old. That was old enough to do difficult things. I was old enough to take care of my elderly, demented mother, but I couldn't ... or wouldn't.

I asked the aide how Mom had been doing and the she told me what I already knew. Mom was in and out of consciousness, but she didn't seem as agitated as she did when she first arrived.

When Jack asked for a snack, I was relieved to have an excuse to leave the room. Guilt pricked my heart. We had been at the hospice for less than an hour and I was already as eager to leave as I was to get here. Of course, no matter where I was there was no comfort, no solace, no escape from what was really happening. Mom was dying.

When the aide paused to give Mom a sip of water, I stepped closer to the bed and leaned down.

"Jack's hungry," I said loudly. "We'll be back tomorrow."

Mom stared at me, but I wasn't sure she understood me. Worse, I had the distinct feeling that she had no idea who I was.

In the months that followed, I prayed for my mother's death. When my sister's call finally came telling me that our mother was dead, I didn't cry — not then, at least. I had mourned years before her poor, tired body ceased. I cried each time I left the hospital after sitting for hours with her as she thrashed about trying to take off her socks. I sobbed after each visit when she refused to eat or take her medications because she thought my sisters and I were plotting to poison her. I mourned her inability to find the correct word or to complete a sentence. For years I had cried as I drove back to Birmingham after a visit, knowing it could be the last time I saw her alive. For years I had I grieved her and the loss of being known by her.

Of all people in the wide world, it is your mother knows you best — or should. Even though my mother and I were separated by a double generation gap (she was born in 1919, and I, in 1962), she had carried me in her womb. Hers was the first voice I heard. Even if she couldn't always express her feelings or her understanding of me, when she looked at me she saw a part of herself in the same way that today, when I look at my son, I see a part of me. She knew me in a way that only a creator can know her creation, like the God of "Jeremiah 1" in the *Old Testament*, "Before I formed you in the womb I knew you, and before you were born I consecrated you."

The desire to be seen and known is powerful. The feeling of obscurity is one of life's loneliest sensations.

As a child, I cried out for attention. In school, I tried my hardest to get good grades and win approval. As I grew older, I sought the interest of the opposite sex by making myself attractive.

In my professional life, I sought out recognition for my accomplishments and contributions. Ultimately, I've spent a great deal of energy throughout my life trying to get other people to notice and know me.

To be truly known, however, I must show my true self. I must be willing to be honest and vulnerable. To be known, I must know myself. Not the false self, who is funny and self-effacing and congenial, but my true self, my most authentic self, the self who's thrilled to hole up with a book on philosophy or stare up at constellations in the night sky. Lao Tzu puts it this way in the *Tao te Ching:*

"Knowing others is intelligence; knowing yourself is true wisdom. Mastering others is strength; mastering yourself is true power. If you realize that you have enough, you are truly rich."[3]

After losing my mother, I had to get to know myself again and allow myself to be known. Self-awareness is a powerful gift to find after all these years. Returning to my authentic self seemed scary at first, but it was the only way I could find peace. As long as I grasped for something that did not match up with reality, I suffered.

What is true self? An answer comes from a beloved children's book, *The Velveteen Rabbit.*

"'Real isn't how you are made,' said the Skin Horse. 'It's a thing that happens to you. When a child loves you for a long, long time, not just to play with, but **really** loves you, then you become Real ... It doesn't happen all at once. You become. It takes a long time. That's why it doesn't happen often to people who break easily, or have sharp edges, or who have to be carefully kept. Generally, by the time you are Real, most of your hair has been loved off, and your eyes drop out and you get loose in the joints and very shabby. But these things don't matter at all, because once you are Real you can't be ugly, except to people who don't understand.'" [4]

It is easier to be loved when I become real. It may not feel easier at first; and yet, only when I'm my authentic, honest self, am I truly lovable. Anything short of this and you may love me, but your love will be conditional on my ability to keep up a ruse. When I am one hundred percent myself, I know I am loved unconditionally. When I recognize my true self, it becomes easier for me to recognize the true essence of others and love them without condition, too. This is the love that Thich Nhat Hanh calls true love, a love without grasping or withholding.

"True love includes the sense of responsibility, accepting the other person as he is, with all his strengths and weaknesses," Hanh writes. "If we like only the best things in the person, that is not love. We have to accept his weaknesses and bring our patience, understanding, and energy to help him transform."[5]

When I own up to my part in my life's frustrations and resentments, I am finally getting real with myself. I am no longer saying what I think you want to hear, or acting in a manner that I hope will please you. Becoming real is a very important aspect to recovering what is true and healthy in myself — and that recovery couldn't have happened at a more opportune moment. At this point in my life, my hair is thinning, my eyes are weak, my joints creak and I'm a bit shabby, but my sharp edges have been worn smooth and I can no longer be broken quite so easily. I am real, and finally ready to be loved.

Chapter 2: Acceptance

The Take-Back Queen

Long ago, before sprawling shopping malls and big box stores ruled the earth, my mother taught me how to shop. At that time, the best department stores lined Main Street in downtown Little Rock. On very special Saturdays, Mom piled my three sisters and me in her Chevy Impala and we'd spend the day trying to match our wishes with reality.

When I was five, I longed for a pair of lavender shoes to match my hand-me-down, lacy, purple Easter dress. I'm sure I begged for a great many things — a suntan Barbie, a white kitten, an EZ-Bake Oven — but this request was not met with my mother's usual response, "We'll see ..." On the contrary, it delighted her.

On Saturday morning, we drove downtown to hunt for a pair of Mary Janes in the perfect shade of purple. We carried the dress with us to match the color. As the youngest of four daughters, I was thrilled to have my mother's full attention. I grasped her hand as we hurried from store to store searching for the ideal shoes. We found plenty of styles in pastel pink and blue, but lavender was not to be found that season — at least not within our price range.

After hours of shopping, Mom determined we would have to make-do with my black patent Christmas shoes. I cried and carried on so much that she bought me a chocolate bunny as consolation. On the ride home, I gorged myself on its ears and developed an awful stomachache. Yet, despite the unsuccessful outcome, that day I discovered my way into my Mom's heart.

Mom loved to shop; buying, however, was another matter. Hers was an endless quest for a blouse in just the right shade of aqua, or the perfect pair of tomato red, kitten-heeled pumps. Once she procured a longed-for item, it might reside in her closet for a few days before she determined it too dark or light, too big or small, or just plain too expensive. Back it would go, and the process would begin again.

Maybe she just wanted to keep looking, to keep searching for whatever it was that she held in her mind. She only purchased an item with the confidence that, should the blue or red turn out to be not quite the right shade, she could always take it back. Everything was returnable; and she was the Take Back Queen.

As I grew older, Mom and I differed in opinion on most topics, but shopping was our Switzerland, and a safe, mutually gratifying activity. She taught me how to appreciate the hunt, always seeking an item that met our lengthy list of qualifications, including size, color, texture, style and (of course) price. Even after I left home and moved across the Southeast, my infrequent trips home always included a trip to the mall with Mom.

Over the years, I learned my mother's taste and I was able to perform a feat that my sisters could not: buy clothes for Mom that she liked. This talent became my super power. It gave me the rare ability to make our mother happy — or so it seemed. (This was still at a time in my life when I thought my actions could transform another person.) Then one day, my power was taken from me. The gig was up. Kryptonite struck.

By age 85, Mom's health had declined significantly. She'd suffered a stroke and never quite recovered. She took medication to regulate high blood pressure and cholesterol. Her doctor prescribed a low-fat, low sodium diet, which she faithfully followed. She also had osteoporosis, which caused curvature in her spine and compressed discs.

On this particular visit, it had been six months since I'd last seen my mom. I bent down to hug her, and felt a new frailty. She relied on a walker to get around, and yet, to my surprise, she still wanted to shop. She said she needed a pair of casual, comfortable navy blue loafers to replace the ones that had become too worn to wear to church. She asked me to take her to Steinmart.

We drove to the nearby strip mall and I let Mom out by the door while I parked the car. By the time I entered the store, mother was already inside, slowly plodding her walker through women's wear. When I caught up with her, she looked up at me as though she had forgotten I was there.

The footwear section was at the very back of the store. Mom moved slowly through the rows of shoes, pausing now and then to pick one up and examine it closer. Nothing met her approval.

I showed her a lovely Bass Weejun loafer in supple dark blue leather with a soft, low heel. I thought it was exactly what she was looking for, but she shook her head. The sole was too rigid; the leather, too dark; the price, too high. I sighed as Mom fingered a bright green sandal. I felt a familiar frustration rise inside me. I was a teenager again, aching to be heard.

At last, Mother found a pair of shoes she liked. Somehow she managed to slip them on her feet without my help. One was navy with a large flower on the toe and the other, black without any embellishment at all.

"Those are two different shoes," I said.

She stared down at her feet, then leaned over and tugged at the flower. When I pointed out (again) that the shoes didn't match, Mom insisted that they did — if only she could get the bow off one.

"They're two different shoes, Mom!" I said again, curtly.

"Oh, let's just go home!" she said in a disgusted tone.

That day, as we left the store with our mission incomplete, I felt cheated. A small, selfish part of me didn't fully comprehend what was happening, but I didn't want our time together to end this way.

Outside the store, I left Mom on the sidewalk while I brought the car around. As I drove near, I saw an old lady with gray, wispy hair, stooped shoulders and bony fingers grasping the handles of her metal walker. I strained to recognize the woman I knew. I realized my foolish hope: to connect with a person who was no longer there. That day I lost a part of my Mom I loved dearly. I lost the Take Back Queen.

Over the next two years, the mother I knew slowly disappeared as her dementia worsened. She spent her final months languishing in a hospice bed. The last time I visited her there I held her hand. Before I left, I told her I loved her. She stared at me, but could not speak.

When Mom passed away, I discovered what all super heroes must learn: With great power comes great responsibility. I was required to dig deep and demonstrate my superhuman ability one last time. My sisters named me designated shopper for the final outfit our mother would ever wear.

As it happened, Mom died the first week of May. The Macy's Mother's Day sale was in full swing, but my task could not wait. With head down, eyes averted, I managed to wend my way past the aggressive perfume pushers in Cosmetics. I tried to ignore the cheery department store signs that scolded, "Don't forget Mom!" I arrived in women's wear not quite unscathed.

Some people are clothed in grace by their losses, but I did not wear grief well. An awful thought bubbled up in my brain. A sick, sad, crazy part of me played a little scene in my head where I asked an eager, smiling saleswoman, "Where are your suits for dead women?" just to watch her cheery expression dissolve. Of course, my mother raised me to be a polite, Southern lady and to refrain from saying anything that would make anyone uncomfortable. (God forbid that anyone be uncomfortable!)

My dark humor consumed me. All around, dutiful daughters purchased powder and perfume sets, purses, bright silk scarves and rhinestone earrings for their mommas like nothing had changed at all — because for them, nothing had changed.

When the sales clerk asked if I needed help, I smiled, shook my head and said, "No, thank you." Honestly, there was nothing she could do.

Mom was only five feet tall in her prime, and as she aged, she shrank. I held up a petite size two red, Jones of New York coatdress and tried to imagine it on my mother's frail, wasted body. The last time I saw her alive, she was as small as a child. Although she was never overweight, before she became sick she would have delighted in fitting into a size two. Now, this dress would swallow her.

I spent hours staring at dresses and suits before I selected two options: the Jones of New York coatdress (size zero) and an Anne Klein crepe suit with a peplum jacket in deep, royal blue. Uncertain of which one would look better on her thin, worn-out body, I bought both. Ever the dutiful daughter and my mother's accomplice, I tucked the receipt into my wallet for safe keeping.

When all was said and done, we buried our mother in the Anne Klein crepe. In it (and thanks to a skilled make-up artist) she looked lovely again. I thought I was dry of tears after years of mourning her loss, but when I saw Mom lying there in the casket, fat tears rolled down my cheeks and I choked out a sob.

In part, I wept because if Mom had been alive, she would have loved that suit, even if she thought it too expensive to buy for herself. (It was marked down 50-percent, which would have pleased her.) Mostly I cried because there were so many times I'd been impatient with my mother — especially when her disease was so very difficult to bear. I mourned the things I did and said that could never be taken back.

Weeks later, I found the strength to complete my duties on behalf of my mother. Yes, I had one more job to do. I took the coatdress back to Macy's for a full refund.

The sick, sad part of me thought of explaining the reason for the return to the sales clerk. Thankfully, she didn't ask why the red Jones of New York didn't work out. If she had asked, I might not have been so very polite. I might have told the truth and not regretted it.

I can't take back my past actions. They are mine to own. Everyday I have opportunities to amend the wrongs of my past, by choosing to embrace a healthier approach to life. It's not easy but the returns are great.

The Worst Best Day

In the fall of 2009, powers far greater than me conspired to change the trajectory of my life. In less than twelve months, my career, family, home and outlook would be very, very different. Of course, I didn't realize it at the time. No. I could not have seen it coming.

It all began with a simple phone call from my sister, Mary, on a balmy Saturday in late October. Our father had been found on the floor of his apartment. He suffered a stroke. Mary gently told me that Dad was conscious and seemed okay, but the neurologist was not sure yet the extent of the damage. Dad had some paralysis on his right side. He could talk, but had trouble finding the words to express himself. For our verbose father this was indeed a setback. Still, Mary's tone was optimistic.

"No need to rush to Little Rock right away" she said. "Dad's stable and he'll be in the hospital for a while."

We had been through this before. Three years ago Dad suffered a heart attack and was given three months to live. Obviously, our father wasn't impressed by the cardiologist's diagnosis. After those three months were up, he was kicked out of Hospice Home for being too healthy.

To be quite honest, when I received that fated phone call, my first thought was not for the well being of my father. I quite expected him to live forever. No, my first thought was singularly more selfish and practical: This was the worst possible week to take off from my job.

For the past three years, I'd been working as an editor for a division of Time. My little editorial group was set up in Birmingham as a cost-savings satellite to the New York publishing mothership. Although the endless deadlines and corporate machinations were stressful, I liked my job and my colleagues. After years as a freelancer, I thought I found the perfect position that combined my creative talents with my experience in marketing and advertising. In exchange for 60 or so hours a week, I collected a nice paycheck, had a healthy 401K piling up and received excellent health insurance for my family.

To land a publishing job in Birmingham, Alabama was no small feat — let alone one with Time. My work ethic and abilities were rewarded, and I'd been promoted to deputy editor. As I edged towards age 50, I appreciated this position even more. I lulled myself into believing I might enjoy this job for years to come — then 2008 happened.

After the mortgage crisis hit, economic woes chipped away at the already vulnerable publishing industry. Advertising revenues continued to drop, while circulation and readership dwindled. Online media was cheap and provided immediate gratification for both advertisers and consumers. The writing was on the wall for anyone who cared to read it.

The previous year, when Time's axe dropped, my little team survived the mayhem. Tucked safely in our southern outpost, I thought we might be spared from the latest onslaught — out of sight, out of mind. But that October rumors drifted down from New York that more jobs would be cut.

As the days ticked down toward November, whispers and closed-door meetings sent waves of paranoia and panic through the ranks from Manhattan to Birmingham. I tried not to worry, sought counsel from those who might know what was going on, and focused on the work at hand. We had magazines to produce and deadlines to meet, despite the uncertainty.

When I received my sister's call I naively thought I would spend a few days in Little Rock to help transition my Dad from the hospital to the rehab facility where he would go for physical therapy. After three years of fielding our parents' medical crises, my sisters and I knew the drill. Dad was a survivor and we never counted him out. Our father lived through battles on Makin and Saipan. He wouldn't dare succumb to something as insignificant as a clogged artery. Of course, I knew the day would come when he would pass away, but I allowed myself to hope that he would recover from this latest medical setback as he had in the past.

The following weekend was Halloween. As I prepared to go to Little Rock, I realized that there was a very good chance I would not be back in time to go trick or treating with Jack. He was seven and loved all things *Star Wars*. I had already purchased a Commander Cody costume, complete with helmet and laser blaster.

That evening, I took Jack to the annual Halloween party at the zoo. We rode the spooky train together, screaming and laughing at all the creepy skeletons and witches. For a few hours I forgot the real-life specters that haunted me.

On Monday morning I packed my Honda and made the six-hour drive to Little Rock. I drove directly to the hospital and found Dad awake, joking with the nurses and even flirting with the physical therapist. Seeing him assured me all would be well. Yet, even he seemed surprised to still be alive.

"I don't know the meaning of all this," he told me. "But I'm beginning to believe that everything happens for a reason."

"Really, Dad?" I laughed. "You're 93-years old and you've just now figured that out?"

He grinned and shook his head.

The stroke impaired his swallow reflex and he was not allowed to eat or even drink water for fear he would choke or aspirate. A feeding tube was inserted through his nose. It was bothersome, and at night, he forgot it was there and swatted at his face, trying to pull it out. As the days progressed, Dad slept more and more, and his periods of lucidity decreased.

I spent the next five days sitting in Dad's hospital room, waiting for doctors and physical therapists to provide insight on his condition. Until his swallow reflex improved and the feeding tube was removed, he could not be released from the hospital.

During the day, I struggled for ways to occupy myself while Dad slept. I checked in with colleagues at the office and answered email. There was still no word from New York about the layoffs — or at least no one would admit to knowing the fate of my team.

"No need to rush back to the office," my manager said. "Take time with your family. There's nothing happening here."

What my manager meant, of course, was, "There's nothing you can do to change the inevitable." She was right. Concern for my father trumped matters at the office, but no matter where I turned, there was little comfort.

During the day, Dad drifted in and out of consciousness. There was little I could do for him except sit by his side. My attempts to encourage him to complete his respiratory and physical therapy were becoming futile as Dad lost ability or desire to perform even simple tasks. When I took his right hand in mine and asked him to squeeze, I only felt faint reciprocation.

Nurses and lab techs came and went, administering meds, taking blood pressure and extracting blood. When they helped him onto the bedpan I turned away. The sight of my father's frail body depressed me. He had always been a strong man, accustomed to physical labor. Even in his 80s, he dug postholes and shouldered 50-pound bags of feed corn. The shriveled, pale man in the hospital bed did not resemble my Daddy, who wrangled livestock and hoisted bales of hay.

In that final week of October, the evenings brought respite in the form a favorite pass time: baseball. Dad and I watched the World Series as the New York Yankees beat the Philadelphia Phillies four games to two.

When I was in second grade, my father introduced me to baseball, and I played on an Optimistic Club ponytail league for years. Since he had no sons, as his youngest daughter (and a tomboy at heart) I found myself trying to fulfill the role by playing catch and swinging an aluminum bat at his pitches. Over the years, I learned a lot from my Dad, the least of which was about how to field a fly ball. He taught me to never give up, no matter how difficult life became. I would come to rely on his lessons in the days to come.

The weekend arrived. Jack went trick or treating without me. Dad's condition was stable, but unimproved. I decided to drive back to Birmingham on Monday. My plan was to return to work for a few days, spend some time with Jack, and drive back to Little Rock the following weekend. By now I had heard that the layoffs would be announced on Wednesday, but there was no indication that my job would be among the cuts.

Before I left Little Rock, I stopped by the hospital to visit with Dad. A male nurse was taking his blood pressure. I stood by my father's side, took his hand in mine, leaned close and kissed his cheek.

"I love you, Dad," I said, trying to smile and not cry.

"I love you too, little girl," he replied, looking me in the eye.

I felt tears well up and my throat tighten. I looked up and the nurse's eyes met mine. We shared a thought in that second, one too sad to speak aloud. I squeezed Dad's hand, kissed his cheek again. Then I left the room, and wept.

As predicted, on Wednesday afternoon word trickled down that layoffs throughout the Time Inc. offices had commenced. I tried to focus on the work at hand, but it was difficult to concentrate. I continued to receive messages and calls from my sisters, who kept me apprised of Dad's condition. He was sleeping more. There was no improvement in his swallow reflex.

Deadlines and meetings that usually nagged for my attention became a welcome distraction. I tried to remain optimistic. Maybe our jobs would be spared. Maybe Dad would be OK. Maybe we would all just continue on in status quo. Maybe.

Throughout my 20-plus year career in media and marketing, I'd seen companies come and go. I'd witnessed departments reorganize and downsize, and jobs become obsolete. Somehow I'd managed to stay ahead of the axe, nimbly jumping from limb to limb as I built my career. I thought I might be immune to this latest "right-sizing."

As the day came to a close, I received an email from the vice-president of our department inviting my staff and me to her office for a morning meeting. As much as I tried not to think the worst, I knew it could only mean one thing.

I drove home that evening, made dinner and helped Jack with his homework. My sisters called to report that Dad was going for a routine test in the morning. We still hoped he might be discharged on Friday. I didn't tell them what was about to happen with my job.

After Jack was tucked in bed, I made myself a drink and sat down to watch my husband work on his latest painting. We talked about my Dad and upcoming plans for Thanksgiving. I didn't mention the possibility of losing my job. I didn't want to speculate and spend the evening mapping out contingency plans. I just wanted one last night of peace.

The next morning I sat in my boss's office and received a white 9" x 12" envelope that contained my severance package. There was no denying reality: My job had been eliminated.

I wish I could say that there was comfort in the fact that more than 600 employees across Time's publishing division lost their jobs that week. There was not. It was very difficult to not take my dismissal from Time as criticism of my talent as an editor and manager.

Although we comforted each other, there was little solace in the fact that my entire team was walking out of the offices together. None of us knew what we'd do next. For all the foreshadowing, no one had a plan B. My colleagues and I worked hard, often spending nights and weekends apart from our families in the name of doing whatever it took to get the job done. For this we were repaid with a standard 9"x 12" white envelope — the contents of which detailed the terms of our severances: a few months salary, COBRA insurance, and instructions for how to rollover a 401(k).

The following day I sat at my desk finalizing layouts for the last magazine I would helm when my oldest sister, Gretchen, called. She was at the hospital. Our father suffered another stroke. There was no defeating the odds this time. I left my desk, walked into a colleague's office, closed her door and cried.

The loss of my job and my father within a 24-hour period seemed unduly cruel. Although in some ways, I was well prepared for my father's passing (he was 93 after all), the one-two punch left me shell-shocked. It was as if the Universe had pulled out all the stops to test my fortitude. In a few months, my marriage would be challenged as well.

Piece-by-piece, the life I had constructed over 47 years was dismantled. I felt ruined. My life certainly did not resemble the one I thought I'd be living as I approached age 50. I'd lost all control, powerless over the economy, my employer, my father's cardiovascular system and my relationships.

I was powerless; and as it turns out, I needed to realize my powerlessness to transform my life. I would learn in the months to come that my father's passing opened me up to take a hard look at my life in a way I could not (or would not) before his death. I would not have embraced Buddhist philosophy while my very Catholic parents were alive. Likewise, I would not have left my 14-year marriage while my mother and father were sick for fear of upsetting them, or worse, disappointing them — again.

Losing my job forced me to seek possibilities that I would not have pursued had I remained in a "secure" corporate job. I wouldn't have taken the time to embark on a journey of spiritual exploration had I kept working 60 hours a week. With the passing away of the ideals I valued most, my life opened up for something much greater. I didn't know it then, but these losses were a beginning, not an end.

The Buddhist parable *The Wise Farmer* illustrates beautifully how viewing life with equanimity can transform any experience.

Once there was a farmer who had only one son and one horse (a mare) to help him work his land. One day the son carelessly left the gate open to the horse's paddock and the horse escaped. When the farmer saw that his only horse escaped, he was saddened but he didn't blame his son. What would be the point? The horse is gone. They will just have to shoulder the plow themselves.

But the farmer had a nosy neighbor, who upon seeing the farmer's plight came by to commiserate. "What will you do without a horse?" the neighbor wails. "Oh, what bad luck!"

The farmer shrugged and said, "Good luck or bad? This is not for me to say."

The next day, the horse returned and she's not alone. The mare attracted 10 fine, wild stallions that happily followed her into the paddock. The farmer's son quickly locked the gate. Of course the nosy neighbor was eavesdropping and marveled at this wonder.

"Oh, my friend! You now have 11 horses! What amazing luck!"

The wise farmer shrugged and said. "Good luck or bad? It is not for me to say."

Soon the son persuaded his father to allow him to tame the wild horses. He jumped on the back of the horse that seemed most docile and was thrown off immediately. His leg was broken in several places. The neighbor heard the screams and ran to see what happened.

"Oh what awful luck! Now your only son will won't be able to help you on the farm."

Of course, the wise farmer responded that it was not for him to judge whether his son's misfortune was good or bad. He took his son to the doctor who set the boy's leg. Although he may have a limp, he would be able to return to work in a month or so.

The following week the farmer was out in the fields when a military officer approached. War had broken out in a nearby province and all the local young men were being called up to serve. The wise farmer took the officer to meet his son, who hobbled outside the house on crutches.

"Never mind," said the officer and he rode away.

The always-vigilant neighbor provided his usual assessment, "Such good luck!"

But the wise farmer simply shrugged, "Is this good luck or bad? Who is to say?"

The wise farmer knew there was more at stake than his son. Perhaps a broken leg kept his child from the conflict, but son's presence may have helped save lives and bring peace to the land.

The wise person, like the wise farmer, is not a color commentator on life, but sees that every outcome holds positive and negative effects. No one can anticipate all the ramifications of any given action. Only a foolish person dares to judge. An American proverb provides the same sentiment: "It is an ill wind indeed that blows no good."

Sure, the deaths of my parents and the loss of my job and the end of my marriage all felt like terrible, life altering losses — and they were. None of these experiences was entirely a loss. All of these experiences yielded healthy outcomes. After all, my parents were very old and had been sick a long time. Their deaths were the healthy resolution of their time on this earth. My job — although lucrative and satisfying in many respects — was also limiting and stressful. The actual loss of my job was very stressful, but it opened new doors for me as a freelancer and provided me with the opportunity to spend more time with my son, and to write my own stories. My divorce opened me up to focus on my spiritual growth — something I might not have done if I wasn't pushed to my emotional limits.

Like the wise farmer, I have to let go of my old habit of judging life's experiences as good or bad, right or wrong, to release

The Nature of Things

my attachment to expectation. If I can loosen my rigid, one-dimensional thinking, I can expand my ability to find contentment regardless of the outcome. In truth, I cannot know the final outcome of any given event as long as life is still unfolding. In my limited perspective, I can only see a part, or point of view.

What I understand about the Divine Nature is there's rhythm, pattern and order, and a general flow to my life, just as there is an order to the seasons or, say, to the life cycle of a flea. But this plan isn't exactly all hearts and roses. Nature's way is not easy, so why in the world do I think my life should be easy?

Yes, life is hard. The first Noble Truth in Buddhist philosophy says that suffering is a part of life because we believe that things will last. According to Thubten Chodron, the word suffering is most often translated from the original Pali wording dukkha, but it means far more than physical or emotional pain. Dukkha is the term for dissatisfaction.[6] By this translation, the primary truth or understanding about human life is that we are often dissatisfied. We want our lives to be the way we want our lives to be and when our lives are not as we'd hoped, we're dissatisfied. We grow attached to our ideas of ourselves and others, and when they change or don't perform by our script for them, we become dissatisfied. All of this dissatisfaction or suffering occurs because we choose to not be present in this moment, in reality.

What if I choose to believe that my life *is* unfolding exactly as it should, just as nature unfolds? Is it possible that if I can set aside my will about how my life *should* be, I can allow my life to unfold in a more natural and divine manner? (I believe this is what 12-Steppers mean when they say, "God's time, not mine.")

If I accept that every minute unfolds exactly as it should, there's no reason for me to judge it and say, "That's not what I wanted right now!" Or "If only this or that would happen now, I'd be happy."

If I believe that what's happening right now in the realm of my experience is **exactly** what I need to happy, there's no reason for me to discriminate. Imagine living life with the faith that whatever is happening — good, bad or indifferent — is exactly what we need to be happy.

If I review my life with a nonjudgmental, objective point of view, I can see that the difficulties I have faced may have helped me attain the gifts that God provides. Sure, there are times when I dissatisfied or disappointed, but on those days I try to remember the words of my father (who was a wise farmer, too), "Everything happens for a reason."

Chapter 3: Surrender

Life After Waffles

Hazy morning light filtered through the frosted panes of the bedroom French doors. Forms took shape. The shapes reminded me that I was in a familiar place, and yet try as I might, I could not remember what I did on Saturdays. No email to answer. No phones ringing. No assignments due. A dull throb of panic settled into my heart. The house was quiet except for the drum of the air conditioner. What did I do on Saturdays before I told my husband I wanted a divorce? After fourteen years of marriage, what was I going to do? More important, how would I find the strength to do it?

    I felt as though I could not place my feet on the floor. For the first time in my life I knew what people meant by the phrase "paralyzed with fear." If I could only remember what it was I did on Saturdays, maybe I'd be okay.

    I turned my back to the morning light. I would go back to sleep until I knew what to do. I closed my eyes. Down the hall, I heard glib strains of the *Sponge Bob* theme song. Life. There was an entire world on cable TV and beyond unfolding without me. Thankfully my son Jack was eight and old enough to entertain himself with the help of Saturday morning cartoons. Jack. What would I tell him? Another wave of anxiety passed through me. What did I do on Saturdays?

"Mom!"

I opened my eyes. Jack stood near the bed in his underpants, his unkempt hair standing on end like an Einstein wig, the effects of summer, neglect, chlorine and a marriage falling apart. His Dad had been in charge of haircuts, but no more.

Jack grasped Panda Ping, his beloved plush toy. After three years of constant companionship, Ping was not so plush. Jack's fingers instinctively found the torn spot on the bear's threadbare arm where the seam had split. Panda Ping's "scratchy spot" was a source of comfort as was his thumb, which he sucked while stroking the bear's split seam.

"Hey honey," I said. "What's wrong?"

"I'm hungry," he said. "I want waffles!"

Waffles! Yes! I make waffles — from scratch — on the weekends. Waffles were something I knew how to do. The thought of waffles reminded me how to get out of bed. Waffles would carry me through the morning until I knew what else I should do. Waffles! Yes! Waffles to the rescue.

Although I know the recipe by heart, having made these waffles dozens of times for Jack, I took out my favorite cookbook. The binding was shot and the pages had come loose. Just like Jack's Panda Ping, the book was worn from loving use. The instructions opened naturally, marked by a dried batter thumbprint and greasy spots of splattered butter.

I combined the ingredients, relieved to have something I could accomplish even if for only a brief time. I tried to stay focused, but I whisked too quickly and a splash of batter slopped onto the floor. I was moving too fast for my own good.

"You do everything so quickly!" Mother remarked when we cooked together long ago. Was that a compliment or a criticism? I could not tell. Her kitchen was too small. Her limited counter space held the toaster and a wooden knife block. We had to use the kitchen table to prepare the meals. How did she manage to make Thanksgiving dinners with dressing and gravy and mashed potatoes and green bean casserole and yellow squash with cheese sauce? Of course, there were pies and cookies, too. Each holiday, she managed to roll out sugar cookies by the dozen.

When we bought our house six years ago, I designed the kitchen with long slabs of counter and an island, too. I visualized the layout at night as I sought sleep, trying not to worry about what was going to happen next. That was years ago. What happened next had happened.

"You do everything so quickly!" Mom said.

Did she know I rushed through life carelessly? Did she worry I would get hurt? Of course, she never spoke of these concerns to me directly. As she was slowing down, my life was picking up speed. On this day, however, I wanted breakfast to last because I was now conscious enough to realize that I had no idea what would happen after waffles.

Breakfast was over too quickly. I didn't have the strength or the patience to load the dishwasher. Yet, that desperate feeling was growing in me again. What now? What do I do now?

I looked out the window. The privet along the back fence had grown long and unruly, like Jack's hair. The little garden where I planted tomatoes was parched, the spindly vines trailed along the ground. The heat has taken its toll. It occurred to me that we could set up the sprinklers and jump through the spray of water like we did when Jack was younger, but I couldn't muster the joy required for sprinkler jumping. There must be something we could do on this long, August day.

I dug through the recycling bin and found a copy of the *Black & White*, a local newspaper. I checked under the listing for concerts or festivals. Nothing. Well, nothing that would interest an eight-year-old boy. I might interest him in a movie if I promised to buy a ten-dollar bucket of popcorn and a seven-dollar Coke, but I wanted to find an activity that would be genuinely fun for us to do together.

Then I saw an ad for the Tragic City Rollers, the local women's roller derby team. I had no idea that Birmingham even had women's roller derby! There was a match that night, but it didn't start until 8 p.m. and the ad said it was two-for-one beer night, which might not be the best time to introduce a young boy to the joys of roller derby. Still the idea inspired me. What else was in this city that I had never heard of? I'd lived here for six years but hadn't really ventured outside my safe suburban trail.

Another thought occurred to me: Jack had never been roller skating. A timid kid, he never longed for inline skates or even a scooter, but maybe it was time he learned to roller skate.

We were in the car on our way to Skates 280 when it occurred to me that it had been almost 35 years since I last laced up a pair of roller skates. I was thirteen years old, flat chested and skinny, with a failed Dorothy Hamill hair cut and aviator-style glasses. I could barely keep my balance and I was too scared to lift both feet from the floor, so I skated stiffly, keeping my left leg stationary while propelling myself with right. My friend Wendy called this stance the "Statue of Liberty." During the Boys' Choice skate I stood with Wendy on the carpet near the lockers as the mirrored ball rained a spectrum of color onto the synchronized couples.

By the time Jack and I reached the skating rink, the temperature had climbed to ninety-five degrees. The cool interior of the skating rink promised relief.

"What if I fall down?" Jack said as we walked through the gravel parking lot.

"Then I'll help you up," I said. "Everyone falls down. That's how you learn."

"What if I get hurt?"

"You'll be fine," I said. "If I can do it, so can you."

I wasn't sure I'd be able to even stand in the skates once they were strapped to my feet, but I was determined to try.

We received our skates and I helped Jack put his on first before I laced mine up. I held his hand as we walked like Frankenstein's monsters across the carpeted rest area. There was a birthday party playing "The Hokey Pokey" in the middle of the rink. The announcer's voice sounded like the skating rink announcer I remembered from my junior-high school days. He cajoled the skaters with exaggerated direction. Jack stood by the partitioned wall and watched the children doing the Hokey-Pokey.

"Let's practice a little on the carpet first," I suggested, and we made our way to the area off to the side near the arcade where only a few kids were hanging out.

Jack tottered along, trying to walk in his skates, only to fall backward onto his butt. I helped him up and held his hand until he was at the partition wall where he could stand. He pulled himself along the wall while I got my bearings on my own skates. I was wobbly, but as I moved one foot and then the other the idea of how to skate took hold in my brain in a way it never had in junior high school. Lifting one foot slightly and striding out while pushing off gently with the opposite leg, I was able to traverse the carpeted arcade area without falling down. I practiced going back and forth a few times, and then went back over to where Jack was still clinging to the wall.

"Give me your hands," I said. "I'll show you how to do it."

I was surprised by the sound of my confidence. Jack tentatively removed one hand from the wall and placed it in mine. Then he relinquished the other. I pulled him out into the middle of the carpeted floor and then let go of one of his hands so that he could skate beside me. I was more or less pulling him along. He squatted low to catch his balance, but he didn't fall back. We practiced like this until the birthday party hokey-pokeyers cleared the skating rink and the announcer invited everyone back onto the floor. I helped Jack over the edge of the carpet and onto the hardwood floor.

The rink was old and the floor, worn, which was perfect for us because it was less slippery. Jack grabbed the railing to steady himself. I took my first steps on the wooden floor and was surprised that my feet stayed beneath me. Was it possibly that after 35 years my balance improved?

I took a few more steps and then carefully lifted my right foot slightly off the floor and stepped forward. Then I lifted my left foot and stepped, propelling myself in an even manner. With the next step, I glided. I left Jack on the rail and made a lap around the rink, and although I had to catch my balance once or twice, I didn't fall. I waved at Jack as I passed him on my second lap.

Over the sound system the announcer turned into a deejay. "All right! Roll on!" he shouted.

A familiar song began to play. "Love Roller Coaster." I laughed out loud. I hadn't heard that song in years. I picked up speed and circled the rink again. Jack was pulling himself along the edge of the rink, his feet slipping from beneath him. I tipped the toe-stop on my left skate to slow myself and stop beside him.

"How ya doing, buddy?" I asked. "Do you want to hold my hand and go around the rink?"

"Okay," he said, "but don't go too fast."

"No, problem," I laughed. I wasn't ready for roller derby yet.

I held his hand and we slowly made our way around the rink together to the sounds of disco songs from my youth. "Y.M.C.A." came on. When the refrain started, the kids circling the rink lifted their arms spelling out the letters just as we did in junior high. I tried to lift my arms to make the Y but Jack clung to my hand as we rounded a curve. He stared at his feet, then turned his face to me and smiled.

"I'm doing it, Mom! I'm doing it!" he shouted.

A blonde girl about his age, but a good six-inches taller, glided by us. She smiled at Jack, then turned around and skated backwards and waved at him. On her next rotation, she slowed near us.

"I can teach him," she said to me.

Jack let go of my hand and took hers. I watched for a moment as Jack teetered along with the girl. When his uneven gait threatened her balance, she let go of his hand, and he fell on his butt.

I skated away, not wanting to stare and embarrass him. This time I rounded the rink with more confidence. The Jackson Five's "ABC" blasted over the speakers. I picked up speed and even began skating to the rhythm of the music. The air conditioned breeze and the throb of the music flowed over me. For a brief and shining moment, I felt happy. I felt that blissful sense of joy that used to wash over me when I was a kid. It was the kind of happy I felt when I was Jack's age and long, hot summer days meant playing for hours in the creek behind our house. Sitting in the shallow stream, I would lift small, smooth stones to reveal an angry looking crawdads, their pinchers extended. I scooped up tadpoles and place them in pools of stagnant, mossy water I created along the slate creek bed. No cares or worries. Just summer days stretched out before me, one melting into the next. They were the longest days of my life. No anticipation, save wondering what was for dinner or what was on TV.

The Nature of Things

I circled Jack and the blonde girl again. She tried to coax him way from the railing. His feet were compelled by the heavy skate boots to slide apart. The girl laughed and called, "Watch me!" Then she pushed away from the rail and glided across the rink, turned expertly and smiled.

"See? It's easy!" she said.

Jack pushed himself away from the railing and promptly fell. I skated over to him and helped him up.

"Are you okay?" I asked.

"Yeah," he said. "Skating is hard."

"It sure is. That little girl must skate all the time to be so good."

"Her name's Callie and she's from Georgia," said Jack. "She's visiting her dad this weekend. Her parents are divorced."

Divorce. The word created a heavy place in my heart. Divorce. Did Jack know?

Callie skated by and Jack tottered after her. I stood at the railing and watched as Jack tried to find his balance. He fell again. Callie turned back and extended a hand to help him up.

Before long, he'd be a teenager going on dates with girls. Before long, he would leave me behind. That ache, the sting of rejection and longing, filled my chest. I swallowed the lump in my throat. I wanted to scream. This was not how my life was supposed to turn out. I was not supposed to be getting divorced ... again.

"And now, ladies and gentlemen, it's time for a couples skate," said the deejay.

Skaters joined hands and moved their wheeled feet to the first brassy strains of Al Green's "Let's Stay Together."

I loved that song, but not today. Deep inside, I felt a familiar longing. I felt that cottony sensation in my throat, stuffing down the sob of a heartbreak that survived 30 years. After all this time, I was still waiting for someone to take my hand.

What was I going to do? I was forty-seven years old, and without a partner. I couldn't continue to cling to the wall in the middle of Skates 280. I pushed off from the railing and propelled myself out into the rink, gliding past Jack and Callie. Jack was falling again, his feet rolling from under his little body. Callie circled him.

Somehow I made it through that day, stringing together one task after the next until it was time to crawl back into bed. As difficult as that time was in my life, I see now the beauty of throwing up my hands and admitting I don't know what to do next. For so long, I always had an answer. I was so quick to give my opinion. I was the fixer, and if I didn't know the answer, I could figure it out. That day, I had no answers. My recipe sustained us only for a time, but for that time, it nourished us.

Hello, Crisis Hotline

The first night of my transition from married life was the most difficult. After we returned home from the skating rink, Jack and I ate dinner and watched a *Star Wars* DVD until it was time for him to go to bed. I did my best to keep to our normal schedule, although normal no longer felt comfortable at all.

We were creatures of habit, he and I. Every night, he requested three stories and then time for "tickle back" and songs. When he was a baby, I made up songs just for him. One was a mash up of the melody "Someone to Watch Over Me" and "Count Your Blessings." It came to me one night years ago as I lie next to Jack in his bed with the lights off after I'd already read stories and tried every other means of inducing his slumber. The words formed in rhymes, the way they do sometimes when I'm not trying too hard.

"Just think of things you like and you'll fall asleep dreaming about them," I said.

There was a verse about Giant Pandas and another about Pokémon. When I sang these songs I felt like a good mother. I gave myself a gold star for originality, at least.

Jack loved his songs and our bedtime ritual, but on this night I was so sad and weary that my voice broke and I began to cry as I finished the last verse.

"What's wrong, Mommy?" Jack asked.

"I'm just tired honey," I said. "All that skating, I guess."

He nodded and said he was tired too. I was relieved to get him tucked into bed. It had been a long day and my patience was wearing thin. My soon-to-be-ex-husband had retreated to the apartment he rented down the street and I was alone in the house. A sick, lonely feeling came over me.

Alone. This is what I wanted, what I had hoped for, right? Peace and quiet. Time to think and be by myself, but somehow it didn't feel as good as I thought it would. The hole in my heart felt as though it were expanding, like a great, black hole in the universe that would absorb everything around it into nothingness. My life felt irreparably damaged.

With Jack in bed, I walked outside to the patio and lit up a cigarette. Someday, I would quit, but not tonight, not while I was going through this emotional crisis. I sat down on the smooth flagstones patio and inhaled deeply before blowing the smoke up to the night sky. It was mid-August and the Perseids meteor was orbiting close to Earth once more, but the show wouldn't start until 3 a.m.

Cigarettes never lasted long enough to satisfy my craving. As I finished it, I thought of lighting another one. Each cigarette separated me from everything I held to be good and wholesome and true — but I couldn't stop myself. I was hooked. I was disgusted with myself, and yet, when the craving became unbearable, I'd sneak away and light up another one.

Back inside the house, all was quiet. I didn't know what else to do so I sat down at my computer. I'd kept a journal since I was

12 years old, but over the course of my 14 years of marriage, I stopped writing down my inner thoughts. Was I afraid that my husband would read what I truly felt? Or was I afraid that if I wrote down what I truly felt, I'd have to admit to myself that I was unhappy?

Dissatisfaction with life had been building for a long time. Yes, things would be good for a while and then I'd blow up. I became so angry at times that I lost my temper over the slightest things. The dishwasher wasn't loaded correctly. Jack failed to pick up his toys. Too much money was spent on a dinner out. Not enough money was spent on my birthday. The litany of slights and wrongs grew and grew. When I lost my job in November, I lost my status as the breadwinner. The next day, my Dad died. I raged about my ex-employer. I raged about the phone company and the Internet service provider and all the atrocities that had been visited upon me by thoughtless motorists and clerks and customer service personnel.

A few months ago I sat in my bedroom, sobbing. I knew something had to change. I must have uttered a prayer. I'm not sure exactly what I prayed for, but it must have sounded something like a plea for help in the general direction of heaven, although I didn't believe in God at the time, not really. I didn't have any type of spiritual belief, but I held onto shreds of my Catholic upbringing and when things got tough, like on that night and I had no where else to turn, I prayed. I don't even know to whom I was praying, but I said something like, "I can't take it anymore. Please help me. Please. I don't want to live like this anymore."

Now, four months later, I was alone. My marriage was ending. My life had changed. Was this the answer to my prayer?

I couldn't sit still. I went onto the balcony and smoked another cigarette, and thought about how ruined my life was now. Yes, it was changing but at what cost to me, to Jack and to my soon-to-be-ex? I took the last drag of my cigarette and threw it down onto the flagstone patio, then I went back into the house, sat down at my computer and typed:

I hate my life. I have messed it up so royally now that it can't be fixed.

I typed out all my fears and anger, my bewilderment, my grief. When I finished typing it was 11:30 p.m. and I could not stop crying. It was too late to call any of my friends, so I picked up my phone and called the Crisis Hotline.

Muriel the Friendly Therapist had insisted I keep the hotline number in my speed dial just in case I needed it. I assured her that I would not get that crazy ... but here I was frantically seeking the number in my phone. I couldn't stop crying or shake the feeling that my life was over, that I was trapped in an impossible situation.

The phone rang only once and a woman answered. She asked me if I was thinking of hurting myself.

"No," I sobbed. "Well, I don't think so. I just can't stop crying."

Through gasps and tears, I poured my heart out to the Crisis Hotline Lady. I told her about my mother and father dying, losing my job and my impending divorce.

"I'm so afraid of what the divorce will do to Jack," I sobbed. "I am just so ... overwhelmed!"

"After all you've been through," she said. "I'd be worried if you weren't upset right now. All that's enough to send anyone over the edge."

Somehow these words made me feel better. Perhaps I wasn't losing my mind. I talked to the volunteer for almost an hour. I talked until I was weary enough to lie down and not have terrible thoughts race through my head. I thanked her profusely and promised to call again if I needed to talk. Nothing had changed, but somehow just being heard helped me get through that night.

On Sunday morning I had trouble getting out of bed again, but this time for a different reason: My legs were stiff. I was emotionally raw from my difficult night, but more than that my body felt bruised from propelling myself around the roller rink like a teenager.

At least my sore thigh muscles could compete for attention with the dull ache in my heart as I awakened to my reality. I was getting divorced — again. Yes, this was round two. Different man. Same me. The common denominator could not be overlooked. The cheese stands alone.

One divorce is understandable. Chalk it up to being young and immature. At age 47, those excuses didn't hold. Now I was a serial divorcee. Great. I was a two-time loser. This was one of the reasons why I didn't want to leave my husband before. I didn't want to admit that I had made yet another mistake. I didn't want to disappoint my parents, and then, after our son was born, I certainly didn't want to let him down.

Jack. He didn't know about the divorce yet. At least I didn't think he did. His father had moved to an apartment two blocks away, which we referred to as his studio. That wasn't exactly a lie since he did use it for painting. And Jack didn't want to know too much. If he noticed that his Dad's side of the bed was made up in the morning, he didn't question it. The less said the better. Soon we would have to have "the talk" with him. A chill of nervousness shot through me, and my palms began to sweat just thinking about the three of us sitting down together to have that conversation.

I took a deep breath. That talk wasn't going to happen today. Today, Jack would spend the afternoon with his dad while I attended another activity I hadn't participated in for years. Thankfully, it did not involve roller skates or physical prowess of any kind.

I took a hot shower and stood in my closet for a while trying to decide what to wear. I was a little nervous and wanted to dress appropriately. The website only specified "wearing revealing clothing, such as tank tops, short skirts and the like is considered inappropriate attire." Beyond those guidelines had had no idea what to expect, but I had made up my mind to go even though it had been almost 15 years since I attended a service. Among all the uncertainty in my life right now, my determination to find a spiritual practice was the one thing of which I was sure.

"What are you going to do for yourself this week?" Muriel the Friendly Therapist asked at the end of our last appointment.

I'm sure she asked this question at the end of most of her therapy sessions. She probably thought I'd tell her I planned to have a massage or go on a shopping spree or have lunch with a girlfriend. My response was not what she expected — especially here in the Bible Belt.

The Nature of Things

"I'm going to a Buddhist center," I said. The words tumbled out of my mouth before I could give them much thought. I smiled. Was that the sound of conviction in my voice?

While his dad took Jack to the pool, I headed to Alabama's one and only Tibetan Buddhist center. As I made the drive across town on that hot August Sunday, I rolled down the window and lit up a Marlboro Light.

Arriving at a nondescript strip mall, I checked the address I'd written down on a scrap of paper. I thought for sure I was in the wrong place. The part of me that was nervous about attending a Buddhist service was ready to turn around and drive to the big shopping mall down the street. Maybe the Buddhist Center wasn't here after all? Perhaps I was off the hook.

Upon closer inspection I saw the name. Nestled between a custom drapery shop and an industrial cleaning company was a glass door with the words *Tibetan Buddhist Center* affixed it. I parked my car, took a deep breath and headed inside.

As I approached the glass door, I saw several pairs of shoes lined up inside. As unlikely as it seemed, I was in Birmingham, Alabama (the buckle of the Bible Belt) entering a Tibetan Buddhist Center to hear the teachings of a Tibetan Buddhist Lama. The fact that there was a Tibetan monk in Birmingham was what my former Catholic self would have called a miracle.

I opened the door and breathed in the earthy spice of incense. Yes, I was in the right place. Incense was a common denominator bridging Catholicism and Buddhism. The familiar fragrance kept me from turning around and getting back in my car.

Was I crazy to look for answers in this strip mall Dharma center? I knew so little about Eastern philosophy, why in the world did I think I belonged here? I was a 47-year-old southerner who should be looking to Jesus for answers — not Buddha. What made me think that prayers chanted in Tibetan would ever mean anything to me? I had never been able to sit still for more than five minutes, let alone meditate on a regular basis. I knew very little about Buddhism when it came down to it. Why did I think it held the answers?

I took off my sandals and placed them besides the other shoes. "I can do this," I told myself.

As I walked around the partition, half dozen men and women seated in simple, straight-back chairs greeted me. There was an older man with a neat white beard, a redheaded girl with a butterfly tattoo on her chest, a tall man who appeared to be in his 30s and an older couple. I smiled and made a small, awkward wave. A woman with dark hair and kind eyes introduced herself as the lay instructor. No one in the room looked vaguely Buddhist.

"We're studying the book, *Buddhism for Beginners* by Thubten Chodron," the woman said. "Grab a copy from that table and join us."

She pointed to a cloth-covered table near the entrance. The beginner book, along with half a dozen other books by the Dalai Lama and other Buddhist teachers were on display. The table also held brightly colored prayer beads, "Save Tibet" bumper stickers, exotic incense in a varying scents, and incense holders. In the middle of the table was a small box where shoppers paid for their purchases. (The Buddhist gift shop worked on the honor system, of

The Nature of Things

course.) Off to one side, a clothes rack displayed T-shirts, tunics with mandarin collars and even a kimono or two.

Another table held a sign-in sheet and pamphlets about Buddhism, copies of the *Snow Lion* newspaper and a large wooden box with a slot cut in the top for donations. There was also a package of Chips Ahoy cookies, an empty tray, Styrofoam cups and paper napkins.

I picked up a copy of *Buddhism for Beginners* from the table and sat down in one of the chairs that lined walls of the simple room. Two stacks of large, black meditation cushions and a pile of smaller pillows occupied one corner. Images of the Buddha in his various incarnations hung on the sunshine yellow walls. This was not the big-bellied Chinese Buddha. Avalokiteśvara (or the Buddha of Compassion) was a svelte, well-appointed holy man with almond-shaped eyes and a pleasant, closed-mouth smile. His hair was done up in a high bun on top of his head and what appeared to be hoops dangled from his ears. (I was later told that over-elongated earlobes were a symbol of the Buddha's ability to perceive the truth.) He wore saffron robes and sat with feet tucked in full Lotus posture. There were other Buddhas depicted on the walls, including the female Buddhas White Tara and Green Tara.

On the opposite wall, a large framed photo of the Dalai Lama smiled down over an ornately decorated altar, which was draped in jewel-toned, silky cloths. On the top tier of the altar, was a large, golden statue of the Buddha, flanked by two smaller Buddha statues. A fourth was seated below the golden Buddha along with a variety of silver bowels. Large vases filled with artificial lotus flowers flanked the altar. A can of Dole pineapple had been placed in front of the altar. Was pineapple somehow significant to Buddhism? They don't have pineapple plants in Tibet. I would later learn that it was a symbolic offering, but on that day, a can of Dole pineapple seemed as out of place on a Buddhist shrine as a Buddhist temple in Birmingham Alabama, and yet, there it was. There I was, not really sure that I fit in, but trying to act as though I might.

As the instructor read from the book, I tried to pay attention, but my thoughts kept drifting. Clearly I needed to practice mind control. My thoughts were leaves on a turbulent stream. I made myself focus by following along the text, tracing over the words with my finger like a child who is learning to read. Finally, Chodron's words cut through my mind's desperate chatter.

"Unaware of our own ignorance, we project fantasized ways of existing onto ourselves and others, thinking that everyone and everything has some inherent nature and exists independently, in and of itself. This gives rise to attachment, an attitude that exaggerates the good qualities of people and things or superimposes good qualities that are not there and then clings to those people or things, thinking they will bring us real happiness."[7]

I felt my throat grow tight and my eyes grow hot with tears. Chodron's words seemed aimed at my heart. Was I divorcing my husband just because I had become discontented? Were our problems so insurmountable that we could not overcome them? Was I just grasping for some sense of happiness that did not exist? I rubbed my forehead with the tips of my fingers to hide my tearful eyes.

The Nature of Things

The outside door opened. The class fell silent as a Buddhist monk in a bright saffron toga appeared at the entrance of the room near the gift shop table. He produced a large thermos from a plastic grocery bag and placed it on the table with the cookies. Everyone quickly stood up, pressed their palms together, and bowed deeply to their teacher. I hopped up a bit late and made what amounted to be a very awkward curtsy. The Lama turned and smiled.

"Please, please, sit down," he said.

Then he looked at me.

"You are new?" he asked.

I nodded yes.

"Welcome!" he said, and he walked over to a chair on the opposite side of the room and sat down.

The Lama was a bonafide Tibetan Buddhist monk who trained at the Namgyal Monastery in Dharamsala, India. Namgyal was the exiled residence of His Holiness Tenzin Gyatso, otherwise known as the fourteenth Dalai Lama. I was now one degree of separation from the Buddhist equivalent of the Pope.

The monk adjusted his robes over his shoulders. His broad countenance emanated a gentle, happy disposition. He smiled and nodded as the instructor told him what we'd been reading.

"The imprints on our mindstream, this is karma," he said and he paused out of respect for this prevailing Buddhist principle. "Very difficult to say ..."

The Lama murmured a word in Tibetan and the chuckled to himself.

"You know," he made a gesture with his hand as though he were digging with a trowel. "Uproot! Negative imprints on our mindstream are very difficult to uproot!"

I smiled at the monk's interpretation, but I felt a dull pain in my heart. Karma. I didn't understand what it meant, but I felt certain karma was at work in my life. What karma had I brought upon myself by asking my husband for a divorce? I looked down at the book in my hands. Perhaps it held the answer.

The Lama checked the time on his gold watch. I didn't know that Buddhist monks kept up with time or wore wristwatches, but then again there was a lot I didn't know.

"Let's have a short practice!" he said, and he clapped his hands together as if we had been trying very hard to make up our minds and finally a decision had been made.

The service lasted about 30 minutes. Most of it was in English and the words were beautiful, but made absolutely, positively no sense to me. I sat on the floor trying to follow along with the prayer book, but I couldn't concentrate on the strange words. At the end of the service, when the Lama stood up, the congregation hopped to their feet and bowed deeply as he walked to the back of the room. I did my best to stand quickly, but my foot tingled and throbbed from lack of circulation and I almost lost my balance. I bowed my head and pressed my palms together. It was not so different from Catholicism after all.

The white-haired man and the tattoo girl followed the Lama back to the Chips Ahoy table. They began setting the little cups on the tray and filling them with steaming chai tea from the Lama's big thermos. Was this Buddhist Communion?

With nowhere else to go on this miserable Sunday, I accepted a cup of tea and a cookie. I wanted to ask the beginner group instructor about Chodron's lesson on ignorance and attachment, but she was talking with the other members of the dharma center. I sipped my tea until the other practitioners began to depart. Finally, I got up the nerve to introduce myself to her again.

"I was wondering if you might be able to help me," I said. "I'm struggling with something."

"You might want to talk with the Lama," the instructor said. "He'll meet with you privately if you want to set up an appointment."

What would a Buddhist monk know about relationships, divorce and marriage? I wondered.

"Um, well, I would really rather speak with you," I said, as my voice broke and my throat tighten. "Please. I think you can help me."

"Okay," she said, seeing my discomfort.

"I'm going through a divorce and I was just wondering ... How do I know if I'm justified in leaving my husband or if I'm just grasping for something that doesn't exist?"

The woman smiled.

"I don't know," she replied, "but the fact that you're asking the question means that you are on the right path."

At first, I felt as though she'd just given me to Buddhist brush-off. I wanted an answer. I wanted a sign. I wanted some definitive indication that I was doing the right thing for the right reason — and I wanted to know right then! Asking questions meant waiting for answers and I didn't want to wait. I thanked the woman and turned to leave.

On my way out, I placed twenty dollars in the box on the gift shop table to pay for my new book. Walking out into the dry, heat of the afternoon I realized that I now knew two things: I had indeed asked the right question; and if answers were to be found, they were within gentle teachings of the Buddha.

Chapter 4: Honesty

Leaving Eden

In second grade while most kids aspired to become a nurse, or a teacher, or a fireman, or a movie star, my career goal was to become ... a saint.

I believed in God, Jesus, Mary, the saints and angels with all my heart. I possessed a child's faith, a true sense of believing without question in something that I could not see or understand. Of course, children are masters at blind faith. (Santa Claus would not have become such a phenomenon if not for their pure willingness to believe.) My parents were devout Catholics and I believed what they told me about God and heaven and hell. I had no reason to question. Before the age of six, I did not perceive any deficit in my life.

Even before I could read, I poured over the colorful illustrations of my *Lives of the Saints* Golden Book. Most of these early Christians were ordinary men and women whose sainthood resulted from being tortured or eaten by lions because they refused to give up their faith in Jesus as the Son of God. Granted, the idea of being tortured or torn limb from limb did not appeal to me in the least, but I did like the thought of being plucked from obscurity by God.

Becoming a saint sounded like being discovered by a talent scout while strolling down the streets of Pasadena. One minute you were a regular girl, and then, in a flash, you were converted into a heavenly rock star. No struggle. No muss. No fuss. Presto! Instant enlightenment! Sainthood was the fast-track to achieving heaven.

You didn't have to become a martyr to join God's divine entourage. In Lourdes, France back in 1858, the Virgin Mary appeared to a group of young girls who were gathering firewood. One of the girls, Bernadette, was later canonized by the Pope. Likewise, in Fatima, Portugal, Mary appeared to three shepherd children. There was a pattern: Sainthood was granted to rural, poor kids. To achieve sainthood in that manner seemed fairly easy and attainable. If Bernadette and shepherd girls could do it, so could I. After all, I lived a humble life on a small farm. We didn't have sheep but we did have cows and pigs. Why couldn't I be like those girls? Perhaps, if I prayed hard and long enough, I could.

Each day during recess while other kids were playing freeze tag and four square, I sneaked into the church on our school's campus. Kids were forbidden to enter the sanctuary without an adult, but I figured that after I became a saint and Our Lady of Holy Souls church was turned into an international pilgrimage shrine, then surely everyone would forgive my trespassing.

Inside the church, I tiptoed to the statue of the Virgin Mary, which was set up on the right side of the altar. In front of her statue, a metal stand held dozens of votive candles in red glass cups. Two velvet-cushioned kneelers were positioned in front of the votives so you could light a candle and then kneel down to offer

The Nature of Things

your intentions to the blue-robed, blue-eyed, plaster Mother of God.

Some saints had a niche or specialty such as lost causes, travel or real estate sales, but Mary was an equal opportunity implorer. For ten cents, you could light a candle and ask Jesus' Mom for help with anything — whether you needed a boost on your math test or to heal your grandma's arthritis. I prayed for many things, but mostly I prayed for a miracle.

When I was certain that the church's ancient rector wasn't around, I quietly set down my Snoopy lunch box and knelt down before the statue. I gently slid a dime into the metal coin box and lit a candle. Then I bowed my head and recited *Hail Mary's*.

After five minutes or so, I opened my eyes just enough to see if the statue of Mary had come to life. Squinting through my eyelashes, peering up at the great saint, hoping to experience a life-changing miracle was a terrifying and exciting moment. Maybe she wouldn't turn into a live version of the Virgin, maybe the statue's feet and hands would begin to bleed with the stigmata or a single, real tear would roll down her plaster cheek. She didn't need to speak to me. I wasn't asking for full-disclosure about how to effect world peace. I just wanted a sign.

Day after day, I sacrificed my playtime to spend time in prayer. And then one day, while I knelt before the shrine of the Holy Virgin, I finally heard a voice.

"What are you doing in the chapel?" the voice asked.

Sister Frances, my second grade teacher, stood over me wagging her finger and shaking her head.

"Children are not supposed to be playing in the chapel!" she said as she pulled me from the velvet kneeler.

I wanted to explain that I wasn't playing, that I was trying to be holy like the saints, but all I could do was cry. Sister Frances escorted me back to the classroom and continued to reprimand me in front of all the other kids. Instead of being praised for my piety and devotion, I was mortified, humiliated, shamed. After that day, the chapel doors were locked.

That very year, in preparation for the sacrament of Holy Confession, Sister Frances taught us the story of Adam and Eve and their Original Sin. Like me, Adam and Eve lived in innocence, playing in the sight of the Creator. Of course, they lived in Paradise with one restriction: No eating fruit from the Tree of Knowledge of Good and Evil. But temptation was too great. After they disobeyed God, they were sent out into the world where they suffered this sense of separation. Their single act of defiance brought all of humanity into a world of pain — or so I was taught.

Not long after Sister Frances banned me from the chapel, I gave up my dream of sainthood and decided to become an archeologist, or a grade school teacher, or a folk singer. Doubts crept in.

One day, I even scribbled heresy in my little pink diary. I wrote, "I don't believe in God." Then I felt so shameful that I scratched through my declaration, ripped the page from the book and shredded it into a million tiny pieces. Once expressed, however, I could not destroy my sense of uncertainty. I still attended church and pretended to believe, but over the years, I separated myself from God.

In college I stopped attending Mass and pronounced myself agnostic. I believed there was something Divine at work in the world, but I didn't believe that God played a personal role in my life.

Throughout my adult years, as I distanced myself from God and religion, I became cynical. I was too smart for God. I was certainly too intellectual to believe angels and miracles. I was never entirely content without a sense of God in my life, but I knew I could not return to the faith of my childhood. Yet, I was haunted by the sense that I had lost something. I just couldn't quite put my finger on what it was.

From time to time, I tried to pray, but I felt like a hypocrite. Although I couldn't name it, I was aware of a deficit and constantly grasped to fulfill that empty spot, what Blaise Pascal describes as a "God-shaped vacuum, in the heart of every person."[8]

This empty void compulsively drew to me whatever felt good and was readily available: Relationships, work, sex, drugs, shopping, anger, control. Of course, none of these corporal pleasures could ever fill my spiritual loss or separation.

Decades after Sister Frances punished me for praying in the chapel, I found myself on my knees asking God for help. My (second) marriage had failed and I felt the loneliness that one can only feel when she is in a relationship where neither party is really present.

One night, I was so unhappy that I prayed for help. I believe that's all I said, "Please help me. I don't know what to do." I did not realize what I was asking God for that night. I certainly didn't realize that if I wanted my life to change, I was going to have to be the one to undergo the transformation.

A few months later, I moved into a one-bedroom apartment a few blocks from my son's elementary school. I was, by turns, excited about this new phase of my life, and terrified of being single again at age 47. Since this was an interim stop along my way to divorce, I took only the furnishings that I absolutely needed: a bed, a chest of drawers, clothing, a small dining table, a desk and chair and my computer. I purchased only two items: a futon bed for my son to sleep on that doubled as a sofa and a small red chest of drawers to hold my meditation shrine.

I never had a shrine in my home before and it represented a new sense of spirituality (that something missing) that would become an important part of my life. Along with candles and incense, I added a statue of the Buddha and the small plastic, glow-in-the-dark Jesus from my childhood. Honestly, I didn't meditate or even pray much in those first months, but the shrine was there as a reminder of what was and what could be.

Over the months and years that followed, as I slowly rebuilt my life, I cobbled together a spiritual practice that made sense to me. It was one part Catholic, one part Buddhist and relied on the tools of 12-Step recovery and the Enneagram to provide me with ways to understand how the Divine is present in my life.

In a way, Buddhism brought me closer to feeling a true sense of God. By stripping away all the labels and limited definitions I placed on God, I could experience childlike faith again.

Today, I can feel the unconditional love of God when I look to the nature that is all around me. I no longer need a miracle to feel chosen; and I don't have to go searching for Eden or Heaven to find what was missing in my life.

"There is no need to travel a great distance to touch the Kingdom of God, because it is not located in space or time," writes Zen Buddhist Master Thich Nhat Hanh. "The Kingdom of God is in your heart. It is in every cell of your physical body. With a single mindful breath, a single insight that is deep enough, you can touch the Kingdom of God."[9]

Selfie

My father fought in the Pacific during World War II as a member of the U.S. Army's 169th Division. He was part of the military operation charged with wresting Japan's stronghold in the islands after the invasion of Pearl Harbor. Before the war, he'd been a farm boy. He was not a tough guy, and he didn't relish going to war, but he did his duty and, thankfully, returned to tell the story.

Although many war veterans shut down and refuse to speak of their experiences after seeing combat, my Dad freely shared his stories with us. The tales were woven into our family's collective narrative. Although they included gruesome topics of death and destruction, Dad often added morals to his stories.

One tale he told repeatedly was about a near-miss. He was marching in the jungle on Saipan and an enemy sniper got a bead on him. At that exact moment, my Dad's intuition told him that he should seek cover — and he did.

"I saw a pile of rocks up ahead of me and all the sudden, I leapt behind them," he said. "At that moment a machine gun opened up and laid down a pattern right where I'd been standing. The fellas behind me saw it happen and thought I was a goner. They were pretty amazed when they saw me walk on into camp. But if I hadn't jumped behind that pile of rocks when I did that day, somebody else woulda been your daddy."

I could not have been more than six years old when I first heard this tale. It was a strange story to tell a child, and yet it made a deep impression on me. The thought that someone else could have been my father was fascinating. Of course, I imagined me as me, exactly the same except with a different man playing the role of my Daddy. I loved my Dad so I hated the thought that I would have anyone else telling me stories and taking me to McDonald's, but I didn't think I would be any different if I had a different biological dad.

Of course, as I grew older, I realized that my very existence depended upon not only my father's DNA, but also on his intuition that day. If he had not survived his experiences in the war, Brigid Elsken Galloway would not be alive, nor would my son. If my father been one step ahead of where he was on that jungle path, his outcome and mine might have been different. There were other lucky breaks too.

In February 1945, his name was selected in a lottery and he was one of six men sent back to the States on furlough. While he was there, the Army began discharging soldiers who had accrued enough credits overseas. The Allies had the Nazi's on the run in Europe and it seemed certain Japan's stronghold wouldn't last. My Dad qualified for early discharge. Had he returned to active duty, he would have joined his division to fight another battle ... on an island called Okinawa. Call it luck or fate or karma or the hand of God, however you want to slice it, my Dad was one lucky guy.

One of my favorite movies of all time is Frank Capra's *It's A Wonderful Life*. Jimmy Stewart (who reminds me of my Dad) plays George Bailey, who at a low point in his life, wishes he'd never been born. A feckless angel named Clarence grants his wish and shows him a powerful perspective. When George sees how many people's lives were changed by his existence, he regains his appreciation for life and his desire to live and face reality again.

In this way, every life — no matter how difficult — is wonderful. When we stop to think about it, our very presence in this world is nothing short of miraculous. There is a Buddhist metaphor that expresses this preciousness vividly.

> "Like a turtle that perchance can place
> Its head within a yoke adrift upon the mighty sea
> This human birth is difficult to find!"[10]

Against impossible odds, I am uniquely present in this life with a mind uniquely capable of achieving self-awareness and (ultimately) enlightenment. Shouldn't I do everything I can to make this life count?

When I start to consider all the causes and conditions that had to align in order for the person who is known as Brigid Elsken Galloway to have been born into this world, I am humbled beyond reckoning. Yet, I take this precious human life for granted almost all the time. I want to be grateful and humble about my very existence, and yet it is with great hubris that I go through most of my life, acting as though I am entitled to be here. When I consider all the actions taken by generations of individuals to bring about my essence to this place and time, I realize a power greater than myself at work in this world.

When I was young, I liked to sneak into my mother's room and rummage about in her bureau drawers where she kept the treasures I coveted: costume jewelry, lace hankies, silk stockings, lip sticks, evening bags and perfume. I was fascinated with these trappings of adulthood.

There was one day in particular I recall vividly. I don't remember what curiosity drew me into the bedroom that day, but I found myself lingering near the large horizontal mirror which hung over my parents' chest of drawers. Standing on one end of the bureau chest, I peered directly into the mirror, and became transfixed by my image.

I looked into my brown eyes and blinked. There was a sense of recognition that I'd never beheld before. The I of my mind, the internal chatterbox, was observing Brigid as a physical being. I wondered at the spark that seemed to reside within my eyes. I looked at the shape of my face and my nose and mouth and pondered the image I saw as though it were the first time I'd ever seen myself. I gazed at the girl staring back at me and was filled with a sense of profound wonder that I existed. I thought, "I am alive! I am ... me. Who is thinking these thoughts?"

I didn't share this experience with anyone until recently. Even now, it's hard to explain. I suppose that day marked the first time I consciously asked, "Who am I?" This is the question we all ask and need answered as we travel through this life. It is the question we ask of ourselves and of God. I exist, but who is the I? This line of self-inquisition will freak me out if I spend too much time considering it. It's like considering infinity. It makes my head hurt.

In the *Old Testament*, God reveals himself from inside the burning bush in the same enigmatic manner, stating, "I am that I am." (Or "I am who I am.") Scholars note "I am" is present tense, indicating that God is present.[11]

After my second divorce, I began to realize that I wasn't a crazy woman who was feeling bored or stuck in her life and simply wanted a change. I had embarked on a journey of self-discovery, but I had no idea of where to begin to find my way back to "I am."

Somehow over the years of my marriage, I had systematically placed much of my authentic self on a shelf. My husband didn't ask me to do this. In fact, we might have had a happier relationship had I not folded up so much of what was important to me and tucked it away out of sight. Why would I do such a thing? Because it was easier than admitting I am who I am.

I have a photo of the little girl who looked into that mirror more than 40 years ago. I know this child was me, and yet I recall very few of my thoughts or actions from that time in my life. Still, I see the same brown eyes — unchanged today even by years of age and anxiety — looking directly into the camera. There is a spark of life that is unmistakable and pure, the essence that is me without shame or guilt or ego or pride or fault or achievement. The more I discover about my essence, the more I will discover the "I am" who is God, the Present and eternal. And the more I discern about the eternal "I am," the more I will know about me.

Chapter 5: Compassion

Tiny Seed. Big Lesson.

In June, Jack and I traveled to my friend Janet's lake house. It was the perfect summer retreat. The cool breeze coming off Watts Bar Dam created welcome relief from the South's thick, humidity. This trip, however, was made more poignant because it was an anniversary of sorts. The previous June, I had driven to Janet's lake house to ponder a very difficult decision that would change the course of many lives. On that trip, as Jack and I made the four-hour drive, I had no idea what would transpire in the months to come. Had I known, I might not have left the comfort of Janet's pleasant home.

This year, the drive zipped by. Jack and I sang along with OutKast and David Bowie and talked about Pokémon. Then he played his new Lego Harry Potter Nintendo game on his DSi while I listened to the news on NPR. In Chattanooga, weekend traffic slowed our pace and Jack grew restless.

"How much longer, Mom?" he asked.

"Do you want me to tell you a story?" I offered. "I heard one called *The Mustard Seed* and I wanted to share it with you."

The Mustard Seed is a Buddhist parable. Apparently, Buddha — like Jesus — sometimes imparted his wisdom in parable form and was fond of condiments.

"Um, not now, Mom," he said. "Maybe later."

Apparently, Jack had heard the *I've got an important lesson to impart to you* tone in my voice. He refocused on his new DSi game where Harry Potter's battle against Lord Voldemort continued. By the time we made our way through traffic, down Lookout Mountain and were speeding north up Interstate 40, we'd both forgotten about the story. An hour later, we arrived at Janet's house.

The weather on the lake was ideal. Hot, but with those temporal breezes that make the warm sun bearable. Janet's two children played with Jack in the water near the dock most of the day; and after dinner they snuggled together, creating a fort in the upstairs loft. Around 10 p.m. the children finally exhausted themselves. Their laughter grew quiet.

I was just falling asleep when I heard a rumble. A storm was moving in, cooling the air and bringing much-needed rain. I peered out the window in time to see a glint of lightning flash across the starless sky. Trees began to sway their leafy finery and, at last, heavy raindrops pinged the tin roof of the cabin.

I snuggled in the soft sheets of the comfortable guest bed and listened for the inevitable: Jack padding downstairs, seeking comfort from the storm. He was old enough, of course, to not be afraid of a clap of thunder or a lightning bolt, but inclement weather provided an excuse to return to a time when he needed me more.

I smiled as he appeared in the doorway. I knew the days were numbered when I could count on him to seek me out during thunder rumbles, and I thanked the stormy night for giving me this sweet gift. I wrapped my arms around him as he snuggled close. But before I could doze off, I heard Jack say another soon to be extinct phrase: "Mom? Will you tell me a story?"

"A story?" I asked. "What kind of story?"

"The story you promised to tell me in the car," he answered.

I smiled and set aside my own desire for sleep. Then I remembered that the story of *The Mustard Seed* was not exactly a comforting bedtime tale, but I was too drowsy to think up another story.

"More than two thousand years ago, in the time of Buddha, mustard was a very popular spice. It wasn't like the bright yellow stuff we put on hot dogs —"

"I hate hot dogs," Jack interrupted. "And I don't like mustard."

"I know, I know," I said, "but many people do like it, and the point is that at that time two thousand years ago, everyone used mustard like we use salt and pepper, okay?"

I felt Jack nod his head.

"I'm telling you this because it's important to understand that everyone, rich or poor, at this period of time in India had mustard seeds into their homes, just as everyone has salt today," I continued.

"So at this time, in a small village in India, a young mother was mourning the loss of her daughter. She was inconsolable because she loved the child so very much and she could not bear the pain. For months the mother sobbed, until one day, a neighbor took pity on her and told her a secret.

'You should seek out the Buddha,' the neighbor told her.

'Can he return my child to me?' the young mother asked.

The neighbor looked at the woman and smiled, 'It is said that he knows the secret to end suffering.'

So the young mother wiped the tears from her eyes and rushed off to find the Buddha. For the first time in months, she was filled with hope that she might be relieved from her despair. Why had she not thought of this before? Surely this wise, holy man could bring her child back to her. For days she traveled and finally she came to the village where the Buddha lived. Upon seeing him, she prostrated before him."

"She pro- what?" asked Jack. (At least I knew he was listening.)

"Prostrated. It means she knelt down before the Buddha as a sign of respect, and touched her forehead to the ground."

"Oooh," said Jack. "Keep going. What happened next?"

"Well, the young mother poured out her sorrow to the Buddha, explaining that her only child had passed from this life and she could not go on without her. The Buddha listened and nodded.

'Please, Master Buddha, it is said you know the way to end my suffering,' she said. 'Please help me! Can you bring my daughter back to me?'

The Buddha smiled his beatific smile and took her hands in his, looking into her eyes.

'I can help you,' he said, 'but you must perform a task for me without question.'

The mother agreed at once to follow the Buddha's instruction.

'Very well,' said the Buddha. 'You must go to every home in this village, and gather a single mustard seed from all those households who have not known death and experienced its pain and loss. Bring me one mustard seed and I will restore your happiness.'

'Of course!' said the young mother. 'I will begin right away and return with what you request.'

She clapped her hands thinking of how easy it would be to find a single mustard seed among all the homes in this large village. Surely it would not be long before she was reunited with her daughter, happy again. She set off, going from house to house, asking everyone she met if they had experienced the pain and loss of death.

The mother knocked on dozens of doors that first day, and the answer was always the same. Some had lost a mother or father or grandfather or sibling. Others had lost a friend or cousin. Each day, the young mother continued on her task, and as the weeks went by, she had still not collected a single, tiny mustard seed. She went to grand homes and modest shacks, but the answer was always the same. No one she met could tell her that he or she had not experienced loss and sorrow.

On she continued, rising early each day and continuing until dark, walking from household to household, asking the same question, and receiving the same answer, never collecting a single mustard seed.

After twelve months, she had visited each and every home and still she was empty handed. But in the process something miraculous happened. As she talked with mothers and fathers and sons and daughters and aunts and uncles about the loved ones they'd lost, the failures they experienced and hardships they faced, she felt the sharp pain of her despair lessen. Often she found herself comforting the people with whom she spoke, sharing the story of her own precious daughter.

After she visited the last home in the village, she returned to the Buddha.

'Have you brought me a mustard seed?' he asked.

'No, Lord Buddha,' the young mother said. 'I have been to every home in this village and not one household has been spared the suffering of loss. I return to you with empty hands.'

The Buddha looked into the woman's dry, clear eyes and smiled.

'What have you found?' he asked.

'Death touches all,' she said. 'Everyone experiences loss and grief, but life continues on.'

And with that realization, the young mother felt a sense of peace and resilience. She returned to her home empty handed, but with a full heart. By setting aside her own pain and considering the suffering of others, she found her cure: loving-kindness and compassion."

As my voice trailed off, I heard Jack's gentle, even breathing. The thunder had subsided, and the downpour, gentled. I closed my eyes to find sleep, but before I could drift off, Jack stirred.

"That was a good story, Mom," he whispered.

I lay there for a time listening to the rain on the roof and the soft, steady inhalations of Jack's breath.

Over the past year, I'd often sought out simple solutions, a simple fix to my problems. Like the grieving mother in Buddha's parable, in seeking answers, I had not found what I was seeking, but I had found solace from those around me who were also grieving lost dreams. No one I knew was immune to life's hardships and dissatisfaction. No one was spared the pain of loss.

Although my life was far from perfect, I felt a sense of peace with the choices I made. I certainly didn't have things all figured out. I'd pretty much given up on finding the answers in this life. Yet, along the way, the quest was enough to get me through.

Attack of the Killer Be's

Most of the time, I'm not sitting on a pillow in a perfect meditation room, surrounded by tranquility and silence. Most of the time, I'm out in the world. The point of meditation is not to sit in silence, but to practice observing my thoughts and not reacting to them so I can respond with more compassion when I am out in the chaotic, crazy world.

Meditation is a practice for real life — the life that throws all kinds of distracting stuff at me 24/7. So once I can become mindful of my thoughts and the process in which my thoughts arise — my triggers, neurosis, addictions, etc. — then I can (hopefully) start to recognize these adverse conditions when I'm off the pillow and (ultimately) respond in a healthier way when those things (inevitably) happen during day to day life.

I don't have to look far to find ways to apply my meditation practice. When I'm writing on deadline, anything can become a distraction. The other day, it was a fly. Not just your average fly, but a fly about the size of a pickup truck ... Okay, the size of a smoked almond ... Okay, the size of a peanut. Suffice to say, he was a larger-than-average housefly. And he was a buzzy fly. You know the type. Some flies are rather stealth. Then there are the large, greenish dudes who seem to exist only to make noise and annoy. The fly buzzing loudly against the casement windows in my office

The Nature of Things

was of the latter breed. If I were casting the remake of the horror movie with Jeff Goldbloom, he would have gotten the title role of the scientist, post-transformative experiment gone wrong.

"Really?" I said to the fly. "You're going to do that buzzing thing in here? I have a big ol' house you could terrorize and lots of great windows to throw yourself against, but you have to come in the one room occupied by a human and bug the living crap out of me while I'm working?"

"Buzz, buzz," he replied.

"Why don't you go buzz the cat?" I said. "She has nothing better to do."

"Buzz, buzz, buzz," replied the fly.

"Good point," I said. "The cat's not Buddhist."

As part of my mindfulness practice, I have changed my insect smash and release policy. In particular, I have a terrible aversion to cock roaches. They give me the heebie-jeebies — especially the large, winged ones that southerners call Palmetto bugs. Not responding with hatred to their beady little eyes and sick shiny bodies has challenged my compassion for years. Recently, however, I've managed to escort of few of the filthy critters out the door — if the cat doesn't turn it into a plaything first.

Apparently the fly had been talking with the roaches and word was out that the smelly incense I burn in front of the statues of happy Asian men means I don't kill insects on sight. As I watched the fly light on my keyboard and wipe its grime-ridden fore legs together, I realized it was time for more Buddhist practice.

I'd never attempted to catch a fly before, but I went to the bathroom and retrieved a thick white hand towel. I waited until

Buzz stopped flying around and landed on the windowpane, and I covered him gently with the towel cupped in my hand. Trying to get away, he flew into the towel. When I heard him buzzing his muted, pissed-off buzzy sound, I pulled the towel slowly from the window, folding it over the places where he might escape. Then I walked quickly to a window I could easily open with one hand, held the towel fully outside of it, and gave it a good shake. I didn't exactly see him blow me a kiss as he flew away, but there were no fly guts on the towel when I was done, so my practice was successful. It took all of three minutes. Amazing.

Acts of compassion like this one, though tedious, mark a shift in my response to life. Let's face it, it's much easier to stop what I'm doing, catch a spider and release it outside than it is to stop myself from yelling at my ex-husband for some perceived annoyance. If I start with showing compassionate to insects, maybe I can work up the food chain ... eventually.

On that day, I returned to my desk to write, congratulating myself about my fly catching efforts. After a while, I heard another buzzing sound, but this time it was not a big, fat green fly. It was a "be," to be specific, it was a Should Be. It wasn't clattering around against a window. That's not where Should Be's are found. No, Should Be's throw themselves against the nice smooth, surfaces of my mind and try to distract me from my tasks.

You probably know the Should Be's; as in "I should be working right now, but I'm checking Facebook." (That one's rather benign.) Or, "I should be more successful by this time in my life." Or "At my age, I should be happily married and edging towards a comfy retirement," or "I should be a better mother, friend, sister, daughter, person." Those are the killer be's and they will distract you from many a good purpose or intention, if you let them. You can spend the better part of your life swatting away those Should Be's, and they will keep coming back. Unlike the annoying buzzing fly, if you get too close to them, Should Be's will sting you every time.

When this Should Be landed on my nose, and began to buzz on and on about how I "should be working at a real job with health insurance and benefits," I didn't reflexively try to slap it into oblivion. At first, I tried to ignore it, but it just made more noise so I would pay it attention.

"How do you think you're gonna pay the mortgage for this swanky new house on a freelancer's pay? I've seen your accounts receivable statement, you know," said the Should Be.

"I've done this for years," I said. "I work hard, I'm a good writer and my clients love me."

"Well, you should be saving more, you know. What if something happens and you can't type? What if you break a hand or something? You can't just call in sick when you freelance."

"I have savings. I have an emergency fund. I have a financial advisor. Go away!"

The Should Be was quiet for a moment.

"But you've never done this all on your own before," it whispered sotto voce. "You're divorced now. You're all alone!"

Ouch! The Should Be's sting found purchase in a very tender spot. I sat with these thoughts and began to feel anxious and depressed.

Before I had a practiced mindfulness and self-awareness, the Should Be's venom would have made me sick with worry. The poison might have worked its way into my head and paralyzed me with fear about my future. Now, I realize that these worries are useless. Sure I can get worked up over financial concerns, but the reality is the only thing that will help me is to stay on task, complete my assignment, send out another query or follow up with a client who I haven't heard from in a while.

I also realize that these Should Be fears are very familiar to me. I've heard versions of them all my life. They are the self doubts that have plagued me since I was a kid. In fact, many of these Should Be's are very childish concerns. So, like the buzzy, green fly, I need to show the Should Be compassion. I need to show myself compassion. So I talk to myself (and I know this sounds a little nuts) the way I would talk to a colleague or friend who was experiencing self doubt. I meet each of the Should Be's fears with rational truths.

"I've never missed a mortgage payment or defaulted on a bill. I will send three emails today to stimulate some new assignments. Besides, I don't really plan to retire in the traditional sense. Yes, it's true, I am divorced and I don't have anyone to help pay expenses, but I have made a budget and I am sticking to it. I've lived alone before. I will be okay."

Mostly I tell myself that fear is just an emotion. Smashing my fears, like smashing a fly, will only make a mess. Instead I need to gently scoop it up and look at Should Be for what it really is. My fears are the product of limited perception, and as such, are flawed. As long as I stay in the present, they can't hurt me, because where I should be is not as important as where I am right now. If I'm going to believe a perception, why not choose the one that says, "You are doing exactly what you should be doing in this moment"? It might take a little more faith to live in the moment, but it's the ultimate Should Be swatter.

Chapter 6: Presence

Obedience School

Somehow I managed to avoid dog ownership until Jack finally wore down his dad with requests for a puppy. He picked out a mutt from the Human Society shelter and named him Rocky. He was a mixture of God only knows what breeds. The vet's best guess was part Australia Cattle Dog. He was a sweet pup with boundless energy.

Rocky made his home in my ex-husband's backyard and I agreed to help out as needed. He was Jack's dog, but of course, as is typical for kids, the ownership was only in name. Since I knew next to nothing about dogs, when Rocky reached six months old we signed up for obedience class at the local Petsmart. From the first class it became apparent that Rocky wasn't the only one who needed training.

Over the course of our six Saturday morning classes, we learned — with help of dog treats and a blue plastic cricket clicker — how to sit, stay, shake hands and walk on a loose leash. The most useful commands was "leave it!"

"Leave it!" is an all-purpose directive that can be used whenever a dog shows excessively enthusiastic interest in anything you don't want him to approach, such as another dog, or another dog's poop, or a baby with an ice cream cone. With the "leave it!" command, you condition the dog to walk away from that desired thing and sit by your side. This repeated action of returning to the person's side resets the dog's urge to compulsively run after anything and everything of interest. Of course, providing treats each time the dog leaves the coveted item and sits down beside you reinforces favorable behavior. The idea is that, eventually, the dog learns to overcome his distractions by merely being reminded by vocal cue.

After our instructor explained the exercise, she set us loose in the aisles of Petsmart to practice. I thought she was insane. Have you seen the aisles of Petsmart? It's a fantasyland for dogs! We could only walk about two steps before Rocky tugged at the end of his leash. My arm was already growing tired from holding him back from shelves of chew toys and stacks doggie delights.

At first, I was very frustrated. How could Rocky ever learn when there were so many wonderful scents? Rocky tugged this way and that, trying to get at all the wonderful dog stuff. He didn't want to "leave it!" When the instructor stopped by to see how we were doing, she could tell I was a bit (to put it nicely) miffed.

"Can we go to aquarium supply aisle?" I whined. "There are just way too many distractions here! He'll never learn."

"He'll get used to it," she said, smiling patiently. "There are going to be even more enticing smells when you take him for a walk outside. Keep working with him. He's a smart dog. He'll learn."

I was dubious, but to my surprise after a few false starts and stops, Rocky began to catch on. As it turns out, Rocky's love of treats far outweighed his desire to sniff stuff. After successfully walking up and down the aisles a few times, Jack set out an entire obstacle course of chew toys. Rocky was able to navigate around them all without getting distracted.

Each week, we worked on these skills and after completing the six-week course, we graduated from Puppy School with honors. Okay, we graduated. Okay, we completed the course and for that we received a standard paper diploma, but as the trainer warned us, the real work was ahead of us — out in the real world.

Leaving a rubber, squeaky bone lying in the aisle of a bright, sterile pet food store is one thing, but a stroll through the neighborhood supplied an infinite number of opportunities to challenge Rocky's obedience degree. Every two inches there was a new distraction. We didn't get but a few feet down the street before he tugged the leash longingly as he lusted after the neighbor's azalea bush.

"Leave it, Rocky!" I said sternly and clicked the plastic cricket.

As we rounded the street corner, he tugged to sniff a mound of monkey grass laced with the scent of a countless dogs, cats, rodents and God only knows what, but finally he came back to my side to gobble down his treat. After the first few blocks, we strolled along nicely until he encountered the one temptation that no amount of kibble could prevent Rocky from lunging after: grey squirrels.

There must be a million grey squirrels living within a mile radius. Every one of them came out to taunt and tease our poor dog. "Leave it, Rocky! Leave it!" became my mantra. Rocky wanted to run after them so badly; he almost launched himself into the air. Of course, he was tethered to me by his nylon leash, but that didn't seem to matter when it came to all things squirrel. He needs more practice for sure, and the only way to break him of this habit of chasing after these teasing, fluffy-tailed distractions was to spend more time reinforcing the behavior to leave it — no matter what.

Rocky is not the only one who is easily distracted. My mind is often filled with grey squirrels that I desperately want to chase. I am easily sidetracked by chattering discursive thoughts. Some days they lead me to — quite literally — bark up the wrong tree. I can observe this tendency whenever I sit down to meditate, but when I'm not on the cushion, the squirrels in my brain can be much more damaging as they compulsively gnaw away at my positive mood and serenity. I'm going about my day and suddenly a negative or worrisome thought scurries across my mind and I lunge for it. Unlike Rocky, my mind is not on a short leash, so I can chase after that negative idea all day if I don't recognize my thought process and tell myself to "leave it!"

Setting aside anxiety is not easy. Even though there is nothing I can do about a situation (I know I have no power over the person, place or thing), I still want to race after it. My only hope of finding peace is to take my mind to obedience school and learn some new strategies for letting go.

Like Rocky, I must replace my habit of chasing squirrels with the desire to sit patiently and be rewarded. This takes effort and practice and it can't be accomplished unless I am willing to experience life on life's terms. In other words, I can't stay in the aquarium section.

If I want to improve the way I respond to life, I must be willing to experience the real distractions that trigger my negative responses. What's my reward? Something much better than kibble. When I refuse to chase that miserable squirrel-like worry across the yard and up a tree, I gulp down a little peace of mind and the satisfaction. Good girl!

God's Minute

When I entered Mount Saint Mary's Academy for girls as a freshman in high school, a relic of a nun named Sister Mary Matthew taught our science class. She seemed to be at least 100 years old. I feared and loved the ancient nun for — despite her age and her elven appearance — she had a no-nonsense air about her. Of course, she'd taught hundreds of teenage girls over the years, and she knew how silly we were. Although she taught the black and white of scientific theory, she held a love of poetry. She insisted that every girl she taught learn the lines to one poem in particular. It was a verse attributed to Dr. Benjamin E. Mays called *God's Minute*.

> I have only just a minute,
> Only sixty seconds in it.
> Didn't seek it,
> Didn't choose it,
> But it's up to me to use it.
> I must suffer if I lose it,
> Give account if I abuse it.
> Just a tiny little minute,
> But eternity is in it.

At the time, I had little appreciation for the beauty or importance of this simple verse. Ironically, my 15-year-old self felt that memorizing this short, pithy verse felt was a complete waste of time. I had better things to do, such as plan my outfit for the next football game, worry about who might ask me to the prom or daydream about my perfect, grown-up life. Even as I repeated Mays' rhymes, my thoughts were fixed on the future.

Today, I understand why Sister Matthew made us memorize *God's Minute*. Most spiritual leaders and gurus espouse the importance of "being present." Why? Perhaps it is because Divine peace can only be found in the present moment. Certainly my craziest, most distraught experiences occurred when I was not living in the present.

Spiritual guru Eckhart Tolle teaches extensively about the importance of living in the present moment. "Always say 'yes' to the present moment," he writes in *The Power of Now*. "What could be more futile, more insane, than to create inner resistance to what already is? What could be more insane than to oppose life itself, which is now and always now? Surrender to what is. Say 'yes' to life — and see how life suddenly starts working for you rather than against you."[12]

Another word for saying yes to the present moment is acceptance. When I accept what is happening in my life right now and drop my regrets, fears and anxieties, I can focus on what is right in front of me.

Being present is a deceptively simple concept; and yet, difficult to sustain. For some reason, humans resist living solely in the moment. Of course, some people excuse their awful, hurtful acts because they were "caught up in the moment." This is not being present. This sense of being in the moment is acting without thought for what might happen next. Living without regard for the consequences of my actions is quite the opposite of being present.

The Buddhist interpretation of living in the moment encourages fully embracing reality. This means valuing life's positive and negative events with equal appreciation. When I see clearly — without judgment or rejection — what is happening, I can honor the past while being mindful that my current action will have an impact on the next moment. That is true presence ... and it is an incredibly difficult balancing act to see and yet not respond to discursive thoughts or events. Indeed, accomplishing this sense of presence is what might be referred to as enlightenment.

Presence is difficult for humans to achieve because we are biologically programmed to react to anything that appears to be a threat. Best-selling author and psychologist Rick Hanson explores the neurology behind these reactions in his book *Hardwiring Happiness*. Although fear may be the strongest distraction, other emotions also cloud our sense of reality. Hanson contends that we are so used to being distracted that it takes concerted effort to break the habit. We are so accustomed to consider only that which is directly in front of us, whether it is a need, desire or fear, that we often act without the wisdom to discern the chain reaction that will ensue if we give in to that impulse. In our ignorance, we run through the jungle from the saber tooth tiger only to fall into a deep pit or lead the beast back to our cave. We might survive, but it's an existence predicated on fear.[13]

It takes effort to see that the tiger is not chasing me. Every perceived slight, rejection or put-down is not a matter of life and death. When I react with charged emotions, in most cases (baring the presence of a real tiger in the room), I'm not reacting to the situation at hand but to a fear response that was conditioned in me since birth. This phenomenon is also called the Pareto Principle or the 80/20 Rule, the law of the vital few.

When Italian economist Vilfredo Pareto formed this rule in 1906 he was describing the unequal distribution of wealth in his county,[14] but the same equation applies to our banked emotions. A broader definition of the rule postulates that 80% of any chosen output is generated by 20% of the input. In psychology this means 80% (or more) of my emotional responses are carried over from past experience. Only a very small portion of my reaction is a response to whatever just occurred.

In essence, when I am not embracing reality, I gather up my emotions and place them in a bag whenever I become upset. I ignore the real cause of my dissatisfaction or discomfort until one day when I reach my capacity for carrying the load, and I let the entire bag fly. Wham! All the wounds of past events that occurred ten, twenty, thirty years ago may come tumbling out. I won't even recognize this phenomenon if I am not striving for a deeper understanding of myself.

My dishonesty, self-seeking, selfish, fearful and inconsiderate behaviors are rooted in the past and future. When I am present, I am less likely to become caught in these habitual patterns. I can experience life as it is presented to me, without fear or expectation or prejudice. Over time, by replacing my knee-jerk reactions with acceptance of what's actually happening in the present moment, I can achieve a more conscious life.

Of course, being present isn't easy. As a human being, it's not my nature to place full attention solely on what I am experiencing in this moment. Mindfulness practice and meditation help build the muscles needed to maintain mental presence. For me, being present is a goal and one that I'm much better at achieving (as least for brief periods of time) today than I was six months ago. But there are many activities besides sitting on a pillow that allow me to practice presence.

One of the best ways I know to practice presence is to get behind the wheel of my car during rush hour traffic. When a 30-minute commute turns into an hour-long crawl through stop-and-go traffic, I have the perfect opportunity. I can either rail and fume about being late for my appointment; or I can see the situation for what it is: a minor inconvenience that is the outcome of living in a modern age when there are more than 250 million cars and trucks on the roads. If I'm being very mindful and present, I might even spend a few moment practicing loving kindness and compassion for my fellow drivers.

Too often, I hurdle myself through life. When I am forced to slow down, even stop, I am given an opportunity to sit with the sense of being powerless. I am powerless over the other cars ahead of me. I am powerless over the road construction crew. I am powerless over the interminably slow traffic lights.

Ralph Waldo Emerson wasn't writing about being stuck in rush hour traffic when he wrote, "To finish the moment, to find the journey's end in every step of the road, to live the greatest number of good hours, is wisdom,"[15] but the sentiment applies. Every journey — no matter how seemingly insignificant — can be an opportunity to practice awareness and compassion. I believe this why God invented the car.

Like training to become a marathon runner, responding to life in a more positive manner takes effort and time. Often becoming present requires a lifetime of practice. When I am fully enjoying life as it is presented, not weighing out options, blaming myself or others, or comparing myself to another person, I lose track of time altogether.

Remaining present is like learning to ride a bicycle. You try and try, and sometimes you fall down, but a certain point, you realize that you are doing it. You're balanced and moving forward and there is a sensation of effortlessness.

When I was in my 30s I had the distinct feeling that I was just biding my time, waiting for my "real life" to begin. I did not appreciate the life I had been given. I longed for an ideal, for the life I might have someday. I thought someday a big event would happen to kick things off. I'd meet the perfect man, land the perfect job, write the perfect story, and suddenly my life would engage in a meaningful way.

Today I see that my life has been unfolding perfectly since before the first moment I drew breath. There was no one big *ta-da!* Every moment has been essential to every moment that came after it. Just as there was no "start," there will be no "stop."

Gaining awareness of the importance of every moment helps me appreciate all the events happening in my life — even the ones that are unpleasant or difficult. I don't have to be happy about the difficulties in my life, but I can appreciate them, value them, and respect them all the same. Because, just as the wonderful, happy, gleaming moments of success yield progress upon this path called life, so too do the miserable, disappointing setbacks. I can see now that all the years that transpired have allowed me to become entirely ready for the moment I now enjoy. Even when I was at my lowest point, struggling with depression and loneliness, I was becoming ready for the happiness I possess today.

Living in the moment means embracing the entirety of reality. Not just the good stuff. When I respond to negative situations — the loss of my job, the deaths of my parents, divorces, the rejections and failures — with a sense of defeat, I'm limiting my perspective. When I feel let down or even cheated because a situation didn't turn out the way I envisioned with my limited mind, I'm not considering that the outcome might just be better for me. There's nothing unhealthy about feeling disappointed as long as I realize that my adverse emotional reaction is a signal indicating how I'm not perceiving the situation fully.

When I sit in meditation, I practice remaining in the present. The candle flickers. Smoke wafts in slight spirals around the incense stick. I see the Buddha statue and the little glow-in-the-dark statue of the child Jesus that I keep on my shrine. Beyond the window, fat robins nibble holly berries from my neighbor's yard. In the other room our turtle, Jaws, knocks against the rock in his aquarium. All this is happening right *now*.

As I sit, I realize that focusing on what's happening right now doesn't feel as comfortable as thinking about the past. Focusing on the present reminds me of how it felt when I felt as a kid trying to ride our very stubborn Shetland pony, Butterball, who had her own ideas of where she wanted to go and how quickly (or slowly) she wanted to get there. Butterball could walk right up to a tree, place her forehead against the truck and just stand there as if stuck. I suppose, in that situation, she was most comfortable standing in the shade of that tree. That's how my mind works. It goes to the place of greatest immediate comfort and often becomes stuck there.

As I continue to sit, I think about my plans for the day. There is work to do. I need to make a number of phone calls to line up interviews for my latest writing assignment. I have an appointment for my annual GYN exam today at three p.m. Later this week is my son's birthday and among other things, I promised to make cupcakes for his class. I need to go to the store ...

Thinking of the future comes easily too, but it's not as comfortable as thinking of the past. Perhaps the future is less desirable because those thoughts are full of to-dos instead of it's-dones. Anxiety may rise up as I think over my list of tasks to be accomplished throughout the week, but in this moment, there is nothing to do except sit on this cushion and stare softly at the flickering candle. Tibetan yogi and poet Milarepa (1052- 1135 AD) explained this phenomenon beautifully in his verse, *The Six Perfections*:

"For generosity, nothing to do,
Other than stop fixating on self.
For morality, nothing to do,
Other than stop being dishonest.

> For patience, nothing to do,
> Other than not fear what is ultimately true.
> For effort, nothing to do,
> Other than practice continuously.
> For meditative stability, nothing to do,
> Other than rest in presence.
> For wisdom, nothing to do,
> Other than know directly how things are."[16]

As it turns out, doing "nothing" is actually accomplishing a lot. It should be a relief to not consider the past or the future, so why is doing nothing so difficult? In a word: multitasking.

I used to pride myself (and often still do) on how many plates I could keep spinning at one time. Of course, when I worked in the media business, being able to manage multiple projects at once was an essential job requirement. Thanks to the crappy economy and the decline of print journalism, my life has become less harried.

As I embrace my life as it is, I want to appreciate experiences as they occur. One of the ways I accomplish this goal is by trying to be more present in everything I do, whether sitting on my meditation pillow or having a conversation with my son about the nuances of *Star Wars*.

Remaining present is not easy, even for someone who grew up with only three TV channels and a transistor radio. My nature wants to flit from one drama to the next, from one relationship to the next, from one job to the next. With meditation, I can discern how I manufacture busyness so I can effectively ignore what is going on in my heart and soul.

Years ago I attended a retreat at Magnolia Grove Buddhist Monastery where Thich Nhat Hanh led a walking meditation, which is traditional at all of Hanh's retreat sites. Of course, the monks and nuns teach sitting meditation as well, but walking meditation provides a special practice of literally connecting with the earth as you generate mindfulness in each step.

"According to the teaching and the practice of the Buddha, life is available only in the present moment, in the here and the now," Hanh says. "And when you go back to the present moment, you have a chance to touch life, to encounter life, to become fully alive and fully present. ... The kingdom of God is available to you in the here and the now. But the question is whether you are available to the kingdom."[17]

When I sit (or walk) in meditation, or listen intently to a friend, or anytime I am truly present in what is happening, I make myself available to a power greater than me. My human nature wants to focus on corporal pleasures and stimulation, but my spiritual nature calls me to pay attention to the miracle of each moment. When I make peace with *what is* and stop longing for *what is not*, isn't that heaven on earth?

Chapter 7: Humility

Scars

There is a three-inch pale, jagged scar above my left breast. It's visible whenever I wear a swimsuit or even a modestly cut sundress or top. When asked about it, I often tell people that I was in a knife fight, but in truth, I had a basal cell carcinoma removed several years ago. The mole was a tiny flat, greyish spot hardly bigger than the circumference of a No. 2 pencil eraser. My dermatologist didn't even spot it during her routine examination of my skin. She only knitted her brows and took a closer look after I brought it to her attention as something that I thought might be abnormal. A biopsy confirmed my suspicion and the slicing began. Afterwards, I wondered how many other spots she missed.

My skin now bears the karma of too much time in the sun when I was a teenager — back in the good ol' days before we acknowledged excessive sun exposure caused skin cancer. Like most girls my age in the South, I slathered my body in baby oil and tried to deep fry myself, sitting outside for hours at midday.

Today, of course, I regret this nonchalant approach to skin care, and not just for the cancer scares and scars. My true regrets occur when I look in the mirror and note the increasing number of wrinkles and age spots that are expressing themselves across my body at an alarming rate. (Ah, vanity! Cancer is nothing compared to looking like a prune.) But every time I catch a glimpse of the scar in the mirror, I'm reminded of my vulnerability. Many of my actions, let alone the act of living on the third planet from the sun, provide me with opportunity to become diseased. The only recourse to sustain a healthy body is to have the diseased places removed.

Likewise, as I attend to my spiritual wellbeing, I discover an increasing number of defects that require closer attention. I can no longer ignore the areas within my nature that are unhealthy. Just like a skin biopsy, spiritual transformation requires the testing of old ideas to determine what is sound and what requires removal. The procedure to extract my character defects is a bit more involving than a twenty-minute incising — and often it's more painful. Becoming aware and conscious of my actions, both past and present, is often a sobering experience when I think back over some of the harmful things I've done and said.

Yes, the rewards of spiritual growth are awesome and great. Being able to appreciate life in a deeper way is very lovely and gratifying. And yet, it's extraordinarily tough to walk through this world without the armor that I amassed over the years. That's what I'm doing when I slowly begin gaining spiritual awareness. It's like eating a really juicy, sweet, fresh, ripe orange for the first time. It's so good, but it's overwhelming. Your mouth is overcome with the sensations and your salivary glands go into overdrive.

Now that I've gained a tiny bit of awareness about how my actions affect myself and other people, you'd think my life would be a cakewalk. It's not. I continue to adjust my responses and behaviors to make healthier choices, but life keeps changing. So just when I think I've got one negative habit curtailed, something happens to rile up yet another. Some days, I feel like an emotional whack-a-mole game.

Even with as much time and effort as I devote to my spiritual practice these days, I often feel like a fake and a phony because, well, I'm still human. This is the real root of the issue, right? As long as I am a spiritual being in this human form, I will struggle with human limitations.

I have a physical body that is flawed beyond measure from too much sunbathing and smoking and eating gallons of cheese dip and ice cream and drinking way too many margaritas. To use an eBay term, I am no longer mint-in-box. I'm physically and emotionally scarred from decades of life on earth. Whereas no amount of plastic surgery, Botox, holistic vitamins and fish oil supplements can return my physical self to its former glory, I do believe that my spiritual practice can revitalize my essential and emotional self.

The big difference is this: Unlike my physical being, my spiritual being is not in a state of natural decline. It's just the opposite. Maybe that's the nature of life. As the body begins to show signs of wear and tear, soul or mindstream or spiritual presence within us, is able to ignite. In many ways this makes sense.

As long as I'm so concerned with the physical and material world, I can't really focus on my spiritual and essential nature. I have to be humbled physically. I have to be shown the impermanence of my mortal life to finally loosen my attachment to it. As it turns out, Carl Jung, the father of modern psychology, beat me to the punch with this theory by about 85 years ago.

"We cannot live the afternoon of life according to the programme of life's morning," Jung wrote. "For what was great in the morning will be little at evening, and what was in the morning true will at evening have become a lie." He goes on to say that with aging "neurosis comes mainly from his clinging to a youthful attitude which is now out of season."[18]

When I was younger, I was in love with my youth and an idea of success that entailed some degree of fame and fortune (or at least material gain). I don't think this was an evil or even a harmful instinct. Now that I see the fragility of the human condition and how I am never satisfied as a human being, I am more inclined to look inside and seek a deeper purpose and a richer sense of self. Is this egotistic? I suppose in a way it is. That's the part that still remains to be burnished or burned away.

How does real, sustained personal transformation — or change — happen? I'm not certain, but I've had a few experiences with this phenomenon that have yielded clues.

It seems one element that must occur for a profound and lasting shift in behavior to occur involves taking a big dose of humility. The word humble, by way of it's Latin origin (humilis), means "on the ground." By that definition, humility is grounding, that which brings us down to earth, where we touch ... reality.

The story of the Buddha's enlightenment echoes this theory. It is said that upon the moment he had attained a pure state of mind he touched the ground and claimed the earth as his witness. At Magnolia Grove Monastery, prostrations are called "touching the earth" and they are a reminder of how we can come back to the reality, to the home base, of our pure mind at any time.

When I am ready to let go of my fantasyland mindset about any given idea or concept or attachment, I become grounded in reality. I touch the earth and find the truth. This process is indeed humbling because it means I have to be willing to admit that I've gone about my life with majorly defective ideas. When I get called up short on my self-centered motives, the wind gets taken from my sails, and I have to sit with my wrongness. Sometimes this can be felt as shame, but I believe shame is just a way to turn humility into another ego trip — which is ultimately also an error of thought. Buddhists call the practice of becoming grounded in reality Right View; and it's the first step on *The Eight Fold Path*, Buddha's core teaching on enlightenment.

I was first introduced to the concept of Right View at Magnolia Grove during talk given by none other than Zen Master, Thich Nhat Hanh. If someone's gonna tell me that I've been viewing the world through a very limited mindset for most of my life, I suppose Hanh is the person to do it. His approach is so gentle you hardly realize you've been schooled until his soft, lilting voice sinks into the recesses of your mind.

That day, Hahn's dharma talk was about how harmful attachment to our ideas could be and how, ultimately, this "poison of the mind" keeps us in a state of suffering. In his book *Buddha Mind, Buddha Body*, he puts it this way, "The secret to Buddhism is to remove all ideas, all concepts, in order for the truth to have a chance to penetrate, to reveal itself."[19]

Under an enormous tent with 900 Thich Nhat Hanh devotees sitting crisscross-applesauce all around me, Hanh's words penetrated my thoughts. Before that moment, it had not occurred to me that I might be attached to my ideas about how life was supposed to play out. I always thought of attachment as it pertained to relationships or possessions, but to think that I might be attached to my ideas was news. It rocked my world then, and it's still rocking it today.

Buddhism has taught me to look beyond the concept to see what is really there. For example, a wooden chair is not just a wooden chair. It is earth from which a seed was planted, and rain and sun that nourished that seed, and lumberjack who cut down the tree and hauled it to the lumberyard, and the carpenter who selected the boards and crafted the chair, etc. As long as I see a chair as simply a piece of furniture in my home and a place for me to sit, I am exhibiting the limitations of my concepts. Expanding my idea of what constitutes a chair takes some effort, and frankly, it's exhausting sometimes. In the same way, appreciating life for the chain of related events that had to take place in order for any given event to have happened takes effort. Sometimes I just want a chair to be a chair. Ultimately, if I can see all of life as a complexly interwoven, perfectly constructed interdependent union of experience, I am at once humbled and empowered.

Stepping ever-so-slightly outside of one's own perspective to see a series of events in an objective manner is an important milestone in maturation. Our ability to objectify our life stories allows us to let go of some of our emotional attachments to our own histories. As I begin to let go of my idea of what my life was, I can also loosen my grip on my idea of what my life is and should be. Of course, letting go of concepts is a scary action and probably contributes (at least subliminally) to what is widely known as mid-life crisis.

When I realize my attachment to my ideas about my life, I realize I am not my stories. But if I am not my stories, who am I?! I start to see that many causes and conditions had to come about in order for any given event or opportunity to occur in my life. I am no longer the author of my destiny. I am "but a player on the stage." I'm acting out my part, and so is everyone else. Just as without the farmer and the farm hand and the miller and the baker, I would never enjoy a loaf of bread, my life experience is dependent upon all other life experience. This is a humbling thought. And what happens next is where the real transformation of concept takes place.

Once I can see my past patterns and how I arrived at point B from point A, and I acknowledge all the help I received along the way, I start to experience my life in real-time in the same way. I begin to appreciate that everything I do every day is influenced by millions of factors and everything I do everyday influences millions more. It's no longer theory. I begin to live in the story, but it's not fiction, it's reality.

Eventually, I may have the ability to see the patterns arise. Sometimes I may even know where a pattern will lead, because I've been there before and that's where it always leads when I respond in the same old way. I begin to explore how the pattern changes if I shift my response, or if I don't respond. Then I can develop a curiosity about my responses, and suddenly, my life isn't just an existence; it's a fascinating science experiment or a great adventure. I'm longer feel I'm being swept along with the tide of events. I might even develop a sense of wonder and appreciation for how all of life unfolds. I still face challenges and setbacks, but now I have an enriched perspective. I no longer grasp onto the false idea that I'm in control, and I no longer fear not being in control. I can't wait to see what happens next because I trust in my experience, and increasingly, I trust my response to my experiences. (This might be called faith.)

Suddenly, life feels new again, like it did when I was a child. I don't have the burden of limited thinking (i.e.: the way I'm told to think about life — or the way I've habitually thought about life). I'm free to allow life to unfold because I see that everything — even the defects and discomforts — serves a purpose. As Pema Chodron writes in *When Things Fall Apart*, "Everything that occurs is not only usable and workable but is actually the path itself. We can use everything that happens to us as the means for waking up."[20]

The Nature of Things

Growing Up

I was never baby-crazy. While my college friends were all starting their families and discussing the merits of Pergo baby strollers and how to keep their nipples from cracking while breastfeeding, I was working at Turner Broadcasting doing something I called "building my career."

My baby was a job that sent me to New York and LA to attend conferences, business dinners and strategy meetings. In the early 90s, Turner Broadcasting Sales was one of the best employers in the world if you enjoyed great meals at four-star restaurants. A bottomless expense account paid for it all. I was young, pretty and single and I could not even imagine myself pregnant, let alone raising a child. But I left Turner after my thirty-second birthday in part because I also could not imagine what my life would be like if I stayed. I told everyone I wanted to "become a writer," but more than that, I wanted to get married and have a family — even though I had no idea what that really meant.

Six months later, I met the man who would become my second ex-husband. We were engaged within three months of our meeting and married in six. Still, having children was not part of the equation. We were liberal bohemians. A baby would change it all, or so I thought.

I resisted the chimes of the biological clock resounding deep inside me. While my girlfriends hatched two, three or four children each and shuttled them in minivans to soccer practice and the orthodontist, I guarded the lifestyle my artsy husband and I designed. But that clock was ticking. Soon I'd be lumped into the ominous distinction of "mother of advanced age" used by OB/GYN's for their patients who were over 35 and pregnant.

I held the sneaking feeling that I wouldn't be a very good mother. I was very emotional and highly impatient — not exactly qualities you look for in a caring nurturer. I knew babies were a lot of work and I couldn't imagine how I would take care of a child and maintain control of my life. I was such a control freak that I felt I had to keep tabs on everything within my universe: the income, the bills, the groceries, the meals we ate, the trips we took, the friends we visited. A baby would challenge my sense of order with its constant neediness. I knew I could not control a baby, and it terrified me.

Plus, there were the physical challenges of childbirth. I was afraid of what pregnancy would do to my body. I didn't want to get fat and for my breasts to sag and my gut to pooch out. Add to that the white-knuckle apprehension about the physical act of pushing a baby through my vaginal canal. I just didn't think I could do it. I knew women had been giving birth for centuries — mostly without the benefit of an epidural — but the thought of the pain I would have to endure scared me. My friends all talked about how wonderful it was to bring new life into the world, but why would I sign up for that gig willingly?

Thankfully my husband succeeded in talking me into giving motherhood a chance. But I wasn't ready to become a mother until the exact moment Jack was born.

Holding his tiny body in my arms for the first time, seeing his little elven face, and his unbelievably perfect little fingers wrapping around mine, touched my heart as nothing had before or ever will again. My heart was broken open in a way that I didn't think possible. My capacity to love increased by infinite measure. I wept, as many new parents do, for joy. The day Jack was born was the best day of my life.

Two days later, driving home with our newborn son carefully tucked into his Pergo car seat, the gravity of motherhood settled inside of me and rekindled the fear that I forgot was there. A wave of terror washed over me. What if something happened to this dear little infant?

It wasn't just the fear that I couldn't change the diaper on this tiny, squirming, seemingly fragile new life. I also felt an overwhelming sense of dread that this beautiful baby could be taken from me in an instant. Having a child made me vulnerable in a way I had never been before. For the first time in my life, I really had something of value to lose.

What if we were in a car wreck? What if Jack just stopped breathing, or suffocated under a pillow in our bed? I felt raw and exposed and completely unprepared to handle this type of responsibility.

Had my husband not been driving the car, I might have turned around right there and returned my child to the hospital, insisting they had made a very big error in letting him out the door with me. I wasn't certain that I could take care of myself let alone a newborn infant.

Somehow I managed to get beyond this initial emotional paralysis. Slowly, I saw that Jack was resilient and hearty and he came with autonomic reflexes built in just like G.I. Joe came with Kung-Fu grip. At a point, I had to stop reading all the horror stories about SIDS and other horrific things that can happen, and just enjoy my baby. I can't tell you exactly how I let go of those fears, but I suspect it had something to do with self-preservation of my sanity, and the fact that babies are demanding. It's hard to be paralyzed with fear — or be or do anything else — when an infant is squalling at the top of his little lungs for food or a diaper change.

I thought that once I got past infancy I could relax, but I am just as vulnerable today as I was that day in the car when Jack was just two days old. The love of a child opens you up to immense sorrow, as well as great joy. Jack is my great Achilles heal, the source of my weakness, but the older he gets and the further he moves outside my orbit, the more resilient I must become.

Little by little, I lose my child every day. Each day he grows further beyond my grasp, beyond my care, beyond my net of safety. I cannot protect him from the life he will lead. I cannot save him from all suffering. The instinct to protect our young is inherent in all mammals, but humans can become obsessed about it, just as we obsess about everything else. Of course, you cannot go through life paralyzed by fear of loss. Sure, you can take precautions to safeguard your children, but there comes a point where you just can't protect them from life.

Kahlil Gibran's beautiful verse *On Children* reminds me that Jack is not *mine* anymore than the air is mine. Yes, we share DNA. I carried him into this world. I have nurtured and loved and cared for his every need since before he was born, but he does not belong to me.

"Your children are not your children.
They are the sons and daughters of Life's longing for itself.
They come through you but not from you,
And though they are with you yet they belong not to you.
You may give them your love but not your thoughts,
For they have their own thoughts.
You may house their bodies but not their souls,
For their souls dwell in the house of tomorrow,
which you cannot visit, not even in your dreams.
You may strive to be like them,
but seek not to make them like you.
For life goes not backward nor tarries with yesterday."

It's easy for parents to feel their children are their possessions, but that is folly. It's easy for parents to heap all sorts of attachment on their children, too, and that is equally foolish. You can hope and pray that your child becomes a happy, successful person, and you can give them all the advantages in your power to help them turn out that way, but at the end of the day, they will become individuals beyond your reckoning. Although, yes, they *need* you now to provide them with food and shelter and love, all too soon will come a day when they do not need you at all. That is the real gift that children provide us: The opportunity to love unconditionally.

Children seek their independence, just as baby sea turtles instinctively make their way from their warm sandy nest to the tenuous ocean's edge. There is no stopping them. Babies can't wait to become mobile, to rollover, to sit, to crawl, to stand, to walk, to run. It all happens with amazing speed. Perhaps that's why parents sometimes try to slow the process down and end up heaping attachment or expectations on their children to hold them back and weigh them down.

At some point, we must let our children go (hopefully sometime *after* they are fully potty trained, because if any sooner, that would just be disgusting), and become the individuals they are meant to be. Fortunately, this process happens slowly. Letting go of your child, as difficult as that might seem, makes life more pleasant for you as an individual, too.

When Jack entered first grade, I started a little experiment. Each day I walked him to school, all the way up to the door, holding his little hand. At the entrance of the school, I would kiss him on each cheek tell him I loved him, and wish him a good day. The experiment was this: How long will it take for Jack to stop allowing me to walk him all the way up to the school entrance, hand in hand?

We got through first grade without a hesitation on Jack's part. Instead there seemed to be insistence that we maintain our morning drop-off ritual.

We got through second grade, almost. One fine, warm morning, during the final week of school, as we were walking up to the door, Jack started chatting with a friend and dropped my hand. After a few steps, he asked, "Can I walk with Brady?"

"Sure," I replied as I felt a little tug on my heart.

During the first week of third grade, Jack turned to me and said, "After we cross the street, can I walk the rest of the way by myself?"

I paused. It was a block. A small city block (not a Manhattan block), and the sidewalk was lined with tidy, old houses and well-kept yards. I could see the crossing guard at the next corner, right in front of the school, and there were hordes of children and their parents also in route. It was a safe block, as safe as any in this world.

Yes, he is my son in temperament and spirit. He has my nose and my dimple in his cheek and the same silly sense of humor, but he is his own person, too.

I let go of Jack's hand and watched as he ran from me … into his future. I thanked God that we still had many years to really let each other go.

Brigid Elsken Galloway

Chapter 8: Reconciliation

Lighting Up

I never intended to become a smoker. In high school I thought people who smoked were white trash. I detested how my hair smelled when I left a party where people were smoking. No one in my family smoked and I never thought I would ... until the day I lit up my first cigarette.

In college, most of my girlfriends smoked socially or late in the evening while drinking pots of coffee and pulling all-nighters to study for exams. It seemed (sorta) cool to smoke at parties or on special occasions. Yet, my smoking career began in a telling manner: I was alone, feeling sorry for myself.

In my sophomore year, I moved off campus to save money on room and board. My roommate chain-smoked Merit Menthols, but since most of my friends smoked now, I overlooked my previous aversion.

College was harder than I thought it would be — and not just because of the academics, which were tough. I did not consider the stress involved in living on one's own. I longed for independence for so long, but now that I had it, there were plenty of times when I wished someone would just tell me what to do. My parents knew even less about the demands of college. They tried to be supportive, but frankly, they really didn't know what to do for me — and of course, I wouldn't give them any clues.

I struggled with Baby Bio and French conversation lab and with all subjects outside my English Literature major. I also struggled with a growing sense of having less than those around me. Rhodes College was a private, liberal arts school and, as such, attracted a rather affluent student body. Even with a Pell Grant and loans, I was scraping to pay for tuition and books. Of course, I didn't confide this to any of my friends because I didn't want them to know that my family couldn't afford to send me to this college. The reality weighed heavy upon me.

One afternoon, I sat alone on my itchy, plaid Salvation Army sofa feeling depressed about my biology grade, or the boy who never called, or the sorority dues I could not pay. My roommate left a pack of Merits on the coffee table and I took one, set it between my lips and lit it. I inhaled and gagged on the minty smoke, but then I took a shallower puff and kept going. I grew light-headed and lay back on the sofa, as I blew streams of smoke up to the plaster ceiling. I didn't particularly like the taste, but there was something calming about the process.

At first, I only bummed cigarettes off my friends or even random strangers at bars or parties. I told myself that as long as I didn't buy my own pack, I wasn't really a smoker. Twenty-five years later, when I finally asked my doctor for a prescription medication to help me quit, I still didn't think of myself as a smoker. Even then, I could not bring myself to admit the truth — let alone concede that I lacked the power to quit on my own.

The Nature of Things

For years I felt disgusted with myself for smoking, and shameful for sneaking outside to light up while my son watched *The Wiggles* or played with his Nintendo DSi. I hated what I was surely doing to my body and I often woke up in a panic, fearing the day when I developed emphysema and could no longer get enough oxygen on my own. I wanted to quit, but I was addicted.

To appease this addiction, I physically separated myself from my son, my friends and my colleagues. When I visited my family in Little Rock, I excused myself frequently so I could squat behind a bush and light up. While commuting to and from work, I drove with the windows down no matter the temperature, and hoped my coworkers couldn't smell cigarette smoke on my clothes. At home, it was easier to get away with, but as Jack grew older, I knew it was just a matter of time before he caught me in the act. Still, I sneaked around doing my best to hide my habit — and effectively separating myself from anyone I thought would disapprove.

I wanted to quit many times — and tried — but there was always a good reason keep smoking. I didn't want to gain weight, so I smoked instead of eating. I was stressed out because my Dad had a heart attack, or because I'd just spent four hours in the ICU trying to keep my demented mother from pulling tubes from her arms and striping off her hospital gown. My husband and I were fighting, or my son wouldn't pee in the potty, or I was on a deadline. Or I was simply lonely and tired. Life gave me an endless list of excuses to justify my bad habit.

I did have one very good reason to quit: My son.

Before I became pregnant, I managed to stop smoking. After he was born, the lack of sleep and constant worry about an infant was enough to make even a nonsmoker take up the habit. I managed my craving until he gave up breast feeding. At that point, I'd been smoke-free for more than a year and I thought I could just have one "every now and then." Wrong. Before I knew it, I was back up to half-a-pack a day or more. I hated the habit and myself, but I felt powerless.

Years later, after embracing a more spiritual lifestyle, I still couldn't quit. I smoked on my way to the Buddhist center. I lit up a cigarette on my drive home from 12-Step meetings or after a session with Muriel the Friendly Therapist. My physical need for nicotine coupled with life's emotional land mines kept me in thrall to my Marlboro Lights.

Then one day I confessed my addiction to a friend whose opinion I highly regarded. Okay, he wasn't a friend. He was a boyfriend, or I wanted him to be. I didn't want him to be turned off by my vice, but I also wanted to have an honest relationship — which meant no more sneaking out to smoke after he was asleep.

I told him that I felt certain Bupropion could help me stop smoking. I used it once years before but I was reluctant to take it because one of the side effects was decreased libido. (Yes, I was that honest.)

My friend looked at me and gently said, "I've never smoked, but if I was addicted to something that could kill me and I knew I could take a pill and it would help me quit, I'd take it no matter the side effects."

I wanted to argue with him, to defend my foolishness, but all I could say was, "You're right."

The next week went to my doctor, confessed my long history of smoking and asked for a prescription. A few days before my 49th birthday, I smoked my last cigarette.

During that first week, I felt dizzy and even more irritable than usual. When an editor critiqued my work, I grew defensive and began to cry (after I hung up the phone, thank God), even though her comments were reasonable. All my emotional responses were magnified. I was so teary on my birthday that I had to excuse myself from family activities a couple of times just to calm myself. I knew that these were side effects of the medication, but because the medication was causing anxiety, I did not have the ability to think through the feelings rationally.

By day six, I thought I was really going nuts. My head felt as though it would explode, and I considered going off the medication. That night, I sat at my computer reading through the drug information. Yes, it said anxiety was a side effect, but I didn't think I could stand to feel this way for three months, which was the standard course of treatment. I decided to call my doctor in the morning. Then, I actually said a little prayer asking for help.

I was about to turn in for the night when a "Ding!" issued from my computer. It was an email from my friend Jenniffer. We worked together in mid 90s. Over the years we'd kept up, although at times we would go for months without corresponding. When I was going through my divorce, Jenniffer jumped back into my life with great compassion and support.

On this night, she sent a belated birthday greeting. I hadn't told her about my attempt to stop smoking. I was so happy to hear from her that I responded in a flash, relating what I was going through with the Bupropion. A moment later, her reply came flying back to me.

"Stick with it," she wrote. "I took that years ago to stop smoking. After the first week those symptoms will go away."

I recalled Jenniffer bumming cigarettes from me from time to time, but I didn't realize it was a habit for her. I certainly didn't know that she had taken Bupropion. Receiving her encouragement at that moment felt like a little miracle.

I went to bed that night comforted. I wasn't going crazy after all. Just hearing from a trusted friend who had experienced what I was going through made me feel better. Sure enough, two days later — as Jenniffer predicted — the neurotic symptoms vanished along with my craving for nicotine. I still felt the emotional triggers, and was keenly aware of points throughout the day when I would have gone outside to smoke, but without the desire for nicotine, I was able to ignore the urges.

Today I am still cigarette-free, but I could not have quit on my own. I needed a higher power (or two) to restore me to healthy behavior — to sanity. I also needed a little sanity to maintain my healthy behavior.

Smoking was never a healthy or sane response to life. It would only lead to more disease and isolation — and that is the nature of addiction. If an addiction is any repeated behavior that separates you from the healthy people and activities you love, this was certainly my experience with nicotine.

How many times did I separate from my son or friends or family members because my body craved nicotine and I needed to smoke, but I didn't want them to see and be disappointed in me? How many times did I excuse myself from a party or dinner to stand outside the restaurant with the other smoking outcasts so I could puff away at a cigarette to get my fix? How much time did smoking take away from my writing, or playing with Jack, or going on long walks? I lost count over the years, but it was way too much.

Having this experience with nicotine has given me insight into the nature of addiction. Turns out, I'm compelled towards a number of unhealthy behaviors. For one, I see now how my need to control the behaviors of others separates me from my better self. My frustration and emotional outbursts push out all thoughts of compassion and love. My anger and resentment cloud my perspective. My discursive emotions effectively separate me from my better self. When I become angry, I lose my connection with reality. I am cut off from options. All I can see is the blackness of frustration. This too is addiction. It was so deep-seated in me that I did not even recognize it as such, until I began becoming more self-aware.

I still have cravings for nicotine from time to time. The triggers are still there: after an argument with my ex, while drinking wine with friends, or having my morning coffee. The only differences now are that I choose not to smoke, and I have come to believe in a power greater than me — in this case, a God called Bupropion.

Dust to Dust

I don't like housework. I will put off mopping floors and cleaning the stovetop until it reaches critical mass and I can't stand it any longer. But of all the household chores, dusting is the one I like the least.

What is it about taking a clean cloth and wiping it over what appears to be a clean surface only to discover that it's filthy? The process is fascinating. Dust is a total mystery to me, a world unto itself. (Think: *Horton Hears a Who.*) I can easily imagine an alternate universe living on my sideboard. Then again, the thought that my sideboard (and every semi-flat surface of my house) is slowly accumulating an ever-thickening layer of detritus that might contain the particles of God only knows what (skin flakes? dirt? bug excrement?) is more than a bit disconcerting. Honestly, I don't want to know the true composition of dust. The fact that it appears unbidden is disturbing enough. Many a mess I conjure and bring upon myself, but dust exists with the insistence of the tide. I know as soon as I wipe a surface "clean," the specks are reconnoitering. There is no reprieve. The only way to prevent dusting is to have nothing to dust.

When I separated from my husband, I only took the things that I felt had use or meaning. I didn't want unnecessary clutter in my new life. But I did take care to retrieve my books; and books, of course, require bookshelves — which, of course, require dusting.

To dust bookshelves properly, one must remove their contents to get down to the bare, dusty surfaces. Each item must be dusted as well. It is a time-consuming task and one I can procrastinate over for days at a time. I need an incentive to dust, and the best motivation I know for housecleaning is to invite friends over. The threat of having my girlfriends see the life-sized dust bunnies beneath the sofa can turn me into a regular cleaning machine.

Not too long ago, I invited some friends over for dinner and thus set a deadline for thoroughly cleaning my house. Since dusting is my least favorite chore, I decided to get it out of the way. I donned my trusty dust mitt and got down to work.

At first I moved quickly from shelf to shelf, removing photos and bric-a-brac to one side while I wiped the surfaces beneath. I'd gently stroke each object clean, replace it and dust the other side of the shelf. I wanted to work quickly and get this chore over with, but when I came to the shelf that held the collection of tiny, white porcelain cats that once belonged to my mother, I slowed down and gave the task my full attention.

These cats have been in my life for as long as I have memory. The cat band is very old and precious to me. I've been a cat-lover since I could toddle after them. My Mom gave me this ceramic band long before she became ill with dementia. She wanted me to have them because she knew I always loved this tiny collection.

There are six little cats, each wearing a bright orange jacket and little black slippers. (Apparently, musical cats are not required to wear pants.) Together they create an orchestra with a bass drum, banjo, cello and French horn and saxophone. There's even a conductor leading the band, but long ago he took a spill and lost an arm. (I don't recall how it happened, but there's a good chance that I was responsible for his amputation.) When friends questioned his appearance, I tell them he was a war veteran. His remaining hand stretches up high and there's a hole in the center of his fist where a baton should be. The baton had long-ago been lost and from time to time my sisters and I fashioned a toothpick into his hand, but it never stayed and made him top-heavy, so he ran the risk of falling again. At some point I gave up trying to find a baton to his scale and just let him lead the band without it. His band members never seemed to mind.

With exquisite care, I gingerly held each cat and wiped it clean of dust, noting the details of their shiny gold accents and the subtle expression on each cat's minuscule face. This little band had played together for decades without missing a gig. Their beady-black eyes steady on their leader, waiting for his emphatic gesture to strike up a new tune. The drummer bore a stamp on the bottom of his drum, "Made in Japan."

As I examined the cats, I considered the hands that held and painted these little felines decades ago. I marveled at how the precise placement of pigment of little pink noses and shading in the ears showed a careful, loving hand. I imagined a lovely, young Asian woman sitting in the china factory creating these little pets. Did she dream of becoming a great artist someday? Or did she aspire toward other goals? Was she toiling in this factory to provide for her family, or to care for an aging parent? Could she be alive today? Where she is now? Of course I would never know the answers to these questions.

    I moved the cat band to one side of the shelf and wiped, clearing the dust patterns left around their little feet. Then I spent not a little time placing them back together as an orchestra. Should the horn section be positioned on the left or the right of the drummer? The banjo-player was always a little off balance due to some error in the factory long ago. When I set him down, he teetered and fell, but fortunately was not injured. I positioned him so that he could lean against the side of the shelf. After all, he's more than 60 years old and deserved to take it easy.

    I shifted my focus to the next shelf, no longer hurrying through my chore. I began to relish the process and the proximity by which this act placed me with items and memories I cherish: old family photos, a handmade tile given to me as a Mother's Day gift, two wooden animals made by my Uncle John, and, of course, my books.

    The books on my shelves read like a time capsule of my life's journey. There were Golden Books from my childhood (*The Lives of the Saints* and *Sam the Firehouse Cat*); the copy of *Lord of the Flies* that I read in high school, alongside my worn editions of *The Norton Anthology* from my Freshman year in college. Collections of poetry and essays by Naomi Nye, a wonderful writer for whom I house sat the summer after I graduated from college, stood near Tom Wolfe's seminal 1980s work, *Bonfire of the Vanities*, signed by Wolfe himself at a business luncheon I attended on one of my first forays to New York. I had an entire shelf devoted to southern fiction by the likes of Rick Bragg, Ellen Gilchrist and Eudora Welty. Another shelf was loaded with self-help and spirituality titles, including the writing of Thomas Moore, Joseph Campbell and M. Scott Peck. There were two shelves packed with cookbooks of all shapes and sizes, some spattered and worn with use.

As I dusted, I recalled Naomi Nye's essay "Maintenance," which is about housework. I found the volume (appropriately titled *Never in a Hurry)*, flipped to the story and read, "I'd like to say a word, just a short one, for the background hum of lesser, unexpected maintenances that can devour a day or days — or a life, if one is not careful. The scrubbing of the little ledge above the doorway belongs in this category, along with the thin lines of dust that quietly gather on bookshelves in front of the books ... I am reminded of Buddhism whenever I undertake one of these invisible tasks: one acts without any thought of reward or foolish notion of glory."[21]

Naomi knew many things thirty years ago that I am only learning now. Housecleaning can be the work of mindful intention. It can become a sacred practice where I honor my past while remaining present.

Today I appreciate the spiritual practice of maintaining my home. When I clean my house, I am demonstrating my appreciation for the wonderful life I have been given. As I sweep the floors and observe the little piles of dirt and crumbs, I make note of the impermanence of all of life. As I wipe down counters, I consider that I can start fresh at any moment if I decide to amend my harmful habits. As I make my little corner of the world a neater, cleaner, healthier place to live, I can feel I've done my part (however minuscule) to affect positive change in the world. Charity begins at home, right?

Emotional housecleaning works the same way. When it comes to defects of my human character, I may overlook negative traits about myself until they get to critical mass and I can't stand to live with the mental clutter anymore. I have to attend to my own mental hygiene just as I attend to my home. Once I place my issues where they belong, I can bring out the beauty that's been hiding beneath the film of dust and clutter.

Examining my life objectively is a spiritual chore. It must be done if I want to invite healthy relationships into my life. As with dusting, I'm often reluctant to begin this process and will find all sorts of excuses to procrastinate. But once I begin tidying up, I get into a groove and appreciate the very act of cleaning, as well as the results.

Through mindful intention I am placed in proximity with all the actions — both positive and negative — that have accumulated throughout my life. I'm given the opportunity to take stock in my responses. It's a step towards wiping the slate clean and making a fresh start. Of course, like the accumulation of dust, the task of increasing self-awareness is never really done. I must continue to tidy and clean throughout my life. And so my work continues, but it's no longer insurmountable. I go about my chores, one task unfolding upon the next.

Chapter 9: Forgiveness

Christmas Past, Present, Perfect

I always loved Christmas, but it let me down. No matter how I wrapped it, I could never make the season as wonderful in reality as I imagined it. The hype and images on TV of happy couples who bought each other Lexus' tied up in gigantic red bows didn't help.

Christmas is to a codependent is what New Year's Eve is to an alcoholic. It's a holiday minefield laden with triggers for relapse at every step. Let's face it; Santa Claus is just a big fat codependent. Think about it. All he does is give, give, give, but his generosity comes with plenty of conditions. You've got to be good, because if you're naughty, you can kiss that wish list good-bye. Yes, he seems like the epitome of generosity, but really, he's just trying to control the behavior of millions of children worldwide.

Like Santa, during the holidays my compulsion to give and to please others in hopes of getting a desired response kicked into high gear. Each year, I'd make myself crazy with the expectation to create the perfect, fairy tale holiday. Of course, Christmas rarely panned out as I hoped. My unrealistic expectations caused many of my Christmas' past to be filled with anxiety and disappointment as I tried to control every candy sprinkle and strand of tinsel.

In December 2011, I was newly divorced, and settling into a new house and a new life. At last, I could create the Christmas I always wanted with a big tree in the foyer and all the trimmings.

The Monday after the Thanksgiving holiday I picked up Jack from school and we headed across town to a Boy Scout tree lot. By the time we made it to there rain was steadily falling. Thankfully, it was a warm evening. No worry. I was prepared. I grabbed two umbrellas from the backseat, as Jack ran ahead into the maze of trees.

A scout handed me a price list. The trees ranged from thirty-nine dollars up to over a hundred dollars. I asked where I could find the thirty-nine dollar trees.

"They're in the back over there," explained a kindly Cub Scout Master. "Those are the trees with the yellow ribbons."

Jack stood by a stately spruce with a blue tag that towered over his head and mine.

"I like this one," he said.

"Look for yellow," I said, "that tree costs $159.00."

Jack looked at the tree with new respect, and then ran ahead to find a yellow-ribbon tree.

The yellows were in the back of the lot, as foretold. The tallest was about the same height as Jack — not what I had in mind for the foyer of my new home. I had envisioned a stately evergreen, shimmering with lights and ornaments, visible from the street through my windows and lead-glass door. My hopes sank. This was not the tree of my dreams, but I wasn't ready to settle just yet.

"Let's keep looking," I said.

"I like this one," said Jack, petting the fronds of a diminutive spruce. "It's cute and cuddly."

It was times like these I felt unworthy to have this child. He would be happy with the littlest, scruffiest tree. He always went for the underdog, like the Charlie Brown Christmas tree in the cartoon.

"Okay, we'll keep that one in mind," I said, looking down at the price sheet. "Let's try to find the white-ribbons."

Jack sprinted through the trees as I looked for white ribbon trees, which were fifty-four dollars. Not a bargain, but perhaps worth it if they were grander.

Smelling a sure sale in the air, the Cub Scout Master approached us.

"Did ya'll find one ya like?" he asked.

"We're still looking around," I said. "Where are the white-ribbon trees?"

The Scout Master trudged to the other end of the tree lot and pointed to a row of spruces. The first one was stout and full and ... tall. It was the tallest of the white-ribbon trees. Jack ran up behind me and shouted, "I want that one!"

"We'll take it!" I said to the Scout Master.

The rain was steadily coming down now. The Scout Master took off his glasses and wiped them on his shirttail. He motioned to an Eagle Scout, who was standing under a nearby tent, and together they hoisted the tree and carried it to my car.

Only as I drove home with the large tree strapped to the hood of my car like a prize elk did I begin to wonder how I would get the tree into my house. Surely it wasn't as heavy as all that. I couldn't recall what I had done on Christmas' past, before I was married, but then, I probably hadn't bought an eight-foot tree. How heavy could a tree possibly be?

I drove slowly, fearing the spruce would shift and slide off the back of my car. A tree flying off a car into traffic could cause plenty of discordant karma. "I'll figure it out when I get home," I thought, focusing on the wet road.

As if scripted, as I pulled up in front of my house, a man walking his dog in the rain stopped and asked me if I needed help with my tree. (I am *not* making this up.) I'd seen this guy before, sometimes in scrubs. He lived on my street, but we'd never met. His dog was a well-groomed Sheep Dog, who probably weighed almost as much as my tree. I took the dog's leash, and in no time, Dr. Do-Good delivered my prize tree to my front porch.

"It'll probably be lighter once it dries out," he said.

I thanked him profusely and marveled at my luck. Getting the tree to the porch had been no problem; surely getting the tree into its stand and into my house wouldn't be so hard.

The following day, while Jack was at school, I determined to set up the tree so it would be ready to decorate when he came home. But there was a problem. Even dry, the tree must have weighed eighty pounds. I could lift it, but only for a brief time.

I managed to grab it full on and wrangle it inside the front door. Then I managed to lift it into the stand. But once in the stand, I couldn't secure it with those maddening metal tree stand eye-screws. There was no way to hold the tree and tighten the screws at the same time.

While I was contemplating my next move, the tree swayed, swinging its weight and almost tipping over in the stand. I felt it falling toward me, and braced it with both arms. Somehow I found the strength to right the tree, but now I was stuck holding it up. My arms began to ache. I wasn't sure how long I could hold on. The eight-foot tall spruce swayed precariously, threatening to fall.

Fortunately, I brought my cell phone downstairs. Unfortunately, it was on the foyer table about four feet out of my reach. If I let the tree fall, it might damage the tree and my new floors. This was an *I Love Lucy* moment if ever there was one.

Slowly, I maneuvered around the tree to position myself closer to the phone. Keeping one hand on the trunk, I fully extended my arms until my fingertips grazed the phone. I inched it closer. Then, still holding up the tree with one hand, I called my next-door neighbor, Emily, and prayed that she was home. (She's a freelance writer, like me, so there was a good chance she'd be there.)

I put the phone on speaker and waited for the sound of the Emily's phone ringing. The call dropped. I redialed and waited for the sound of Emily's phone ringing. The call dropped again. My right arm, which was holding up the 80-pound tree, began to tremble. I hit the redial button again ... and the phone began to ring. Emily answered right away. She was at my front door in moments, following the trail of spruce fronds and laughing at me for trying to handle this enormous tree by myself. Within about five minutes we had the tree secured in the stand, but there was one little problem: The trunk was hopelessly crooked.

Later that day, Emily's husband came over and placed the tree in the stand so that it wouldn't topple, but nothing could correct the tree's profound scoliosis. It would never be perfect, but at least Jack and I could now decorate the massive spruce.

Opening the containers of Christmas ornaments brought back memories of Christmas' past. There was the little white sparkly bird whose google eyes I picked off when I was just a toddler, and the ceramic Mrs. Santa Claus that I painted as a Brownie Scout in second grade. I also had the glass icicles I bought for my first Christmas tree after I graduated from college and heavy glass mercury ornaments from my first marriage. Another box held a tiny resin bear with Jack's name on it that my mother had given him when he was an infant, and there were an assortment of nutcrackers that Jack and I collected over the years. Each ornament had a history, a story to document milestones of our lives.

One by one, we placed the beloved ornaments on the tree. I decorated the tallest branches, while Jack adorned the lower ones. When we were done, we stepped back to admire our work and proclaimed it the most beautiful Christmas tree ever (which is what we said every year).

We were able to hide the tree's imperfections, and yet no amount of fresh spruce aroma or decorations could mask the reality of this year's holiday: This year Jack would be at his father's on Christmas morning.

For the first time in his life, I wouldn't be peering around the corner of the living room when Jack woke up and discovered what Santa left beneath the tree. And I would be alone on

Christmas morning. As the holiday drew closer, I grew frantic with the thought. How would I make it through the holidays?

Then, I hatched a great idea. The best way to set aside your problems was to help someone else, right? I would throw myself into helping others and forget about my own troubles. I called the local community kitchen and generously offered to help cook.

"I'm sorry," the volunteer coordinator said. "The holidays are already covered. Try back in January."

As it turned out, from Thanksgiving through New Years every church, synagogue, Girl Scout troop and Kiwanis Club in town queues up to cook turkey and dressing for the homeless.

Well, I wanted to give and by God, I'd give! I hatched a second idea. I'd work with a group that was already signed up to serve at the kitchen. There was just one problem: I wasn't a card-carrying member of a church or civic organization. Again I applied my I-will-not-take-no-for-an-answer attitude and formulated a brilliant plan.

Some of my friends attended a nearby Episcopal church that frequently served meals at the shelter. So one Sunday morning, I put on a skirt and panty hose and attended mass with them. (I was raised Catholic, so I can easily pass for Episcopal.)

After the service, while my friends were enjoying fellowship and coffee, I sneaked into the community center and scrawled my name on their volunteer sign-up sheet to serve lunch at the community kitchen. No one was the wiser.

The day to volunteer rolled around and I served turkey and dressing and all the trimmings with my new Episcopal friends. While I doled out mashed potatoes, green beans and rolls to the down-on-their-luckers I tried my best to generate compassion for each and every soul. Seeing their smiles of appreciation, I felt humbled. I realized I really did have a lot for which to be grateful.

My Christmas wasn't going to be ideal, but at least I had a home. I had a family. I had plenty of food and clothes and everything I wanted. The experience left me feeling so good that after we cleaned the pots and pans and put the cafeteria back in order, I asked the cook who managed the kitchen if I could help prepare meals on a regular basis. He seemed happy to have my assistance, and I walked away feeling a little better about my life.

The following Monday, I showed up to help serve the noon meal. I quickly learned my way around the industrial dishwasher and the pantry. The chef seemed to genuinely appreciate my help. Later that day, as I strolled out of the kitchen humming *Kumbaya*, the volunteer coordinator cornered me.

"You're not on the list," he said.

"Oh, well ... I just thought you needed help ..." I replied.

"We have groups that sign up," he said. "It's all planned out for months. You have to be on the list."

"Oh, okay," I said, my face flushing with humiliation. "I was only trying to help"

"I have your number," the coordinator said flatly. "I'll call you if I need you."

I walked away quickly so he couldn't see me cry. I had just been fired as a volunteer at a soup kitchen! I couldn't believe it. I was such a big loser that even a homeless shelter didn't want my help.

As I drove home, my embarrassment turned into anger when I thought of how I'd been treated by the hapless volunteer coordinator. What an idiot! What in ingrate! How dare he dismiss me like that!

At home my anger and shame turned inward as I threw myself an enormous pity party. I forgot all about the women and men who lived on the streets. I sat in my nice warm house and sobbed for myself. I didn't think about the hardships the homeless faced everyday and how lonely they must feel. All I could think about was that I was all alone. Poor, poor me! Rejected again — and by a homeless shelter no less!

I wish I could tell you that I had a revelation right then and there. I wish I could tell you that in that moment of pure self-pity I had a breakthrough, an insight, a glimpse of clarity shining through, but I didn't. I spent the rest of that day feeling weak and raw and burned out. Then I made it worse.

I looked at my Christmas tree and noticed the lack of gifts beneath it. I moped around the house thinking about how I wasn't going to get a single Christmas gift that year. My parents were dead, and my sisters and I didn't exchange gifts anymore because we're grown up people and we called a truce on gift giving years ago. I wallowed in feeling forgotten for quite a while.

Finally, I grew bored with my self-pity and I called my friend Charlotte. I was still hurt and outraged when I related to her what happened with the volunteer coordinator. I was ready to be surrounded in the snug and sticky blanket of commiseration, but Charlotte did the most remarkable thing: She laughed.

Then (remarkably) I saw how ridiculous I had been. A tiny glimmer of light crept in. I began to laugh at myself for being fired from the soup kitchen.

"Maybe he did you a favor," she said. "Maybe that's not what you're supposed to be doing right now."

Charlotte's insight reminded me of a Buddhist saying, "My enemy is my greatest teacher." Certainly the volunteer coordinator was not my foe, but I had been thinking not-so-nice thoughts about him. Yet, maybe I had gotten it all wrong. Maybe, just maybe, he did do me a favor rather than an injustice.

When I hung up the phone, I saw there were dishes piled in the sink. I'd been too busy doing dishes at the soup kitchen to wash my own. After I filled the dishwasher, I swept the crumbs up off the floor. Then I wiped down the stove and the countertops. I made myself a nice lunch of tomato soup and popcorn, just like my mom used to make for me when I was a little girl.

The next day, I felt good enough to change out of my sweat pants and go shopping for Christmas gifts for my son as well as for some children I didn't know whose names I gathered from a local Angel Tree. I even bought a very small gift for my ex-husband. I wrapped the gifts and placed them under my tree.

As the days ticked down to December 25, whenever I felt anxiety's twinge, I memorized favorite Buddhist prayers or repeated a simple mantra. I called my sisters. I sent a quick text to a friend. I took long, hot bubble baths and read dharma books while I soaked in the tub. I said *The Serenity Prayer* until I meant every word.

Somehow I made it to December 24. Along the way, while focusing on the tasks at hand and not on some made-up fantasy, I swallowed my pride and called my ex-husband and asked him for a very special gift.

"Would it be too weird if I slept in Jack's room on Christmas Eve?" I asked. "I don't want this to be awkward, but I really want to be there when he wakes up."

My ex gave it some thought and agreed it would be okay. Jack was thrilled that Mom was coming for a Christmas Eve slumber party. That night, after attending midnight mass, I tiptoed into Jack's room, set aside my expectations and resentments, and climbed onto the top bunk.

Today, I look back on that holiday season as one of (if not the) best of my life. Christmas did not go down at all in the way I envisioned it. It was messy and icky and there was not a new car in my driveway on Christmas morning. And yet I discovered (much like Dr. Seuss' Grinch) that Christmas didn't need to be this way or that to be celebrated.

That season, for the first time in my life, I understood what it meant to let go, not just of a relationship or an outcome, but what it meant to let go — really let go — of a long-held ideal.

Auld Lang Syne

After clearing the emotional hurdle of Christmas, I still had New Year's Eve before me. Jack was with his Dad. I was a party of one.

Fortunately, I had been invited to a fabulous New Year's Eve dinner party in Asheville, North Carolina. I was grateful that my dear friend Kaye and her husband had included me and I was looking forward to attending ... until two days before the fateful the big night. Even though I had no alternate plan, I decided to stay home. In part, the thought of spending New Year's Eve as the eleventh wheel at a couples-only dinner party was just too much to bear. More than that, I was tired and felt the healthiest option for me was to spend the evening in quiet contemplation.

So much had happened over the past few months: my divorce was finalized; I bought a house and moved into a new neighborhood; I had fallen in and out of love half a dozen times. I needed a rest.

I filled my fridge with my favorite holiday snacks, borrowed some good books from the library and settled in for a very different type of New Year's celebration. At home, without distraction, this evening became the optimal time to revisit a prevalent pattern in my relationships. Specifically, I began to consider why New Year's Eve filled me with so much trepidation.

Then I recalled a vivid memory. I couldn't believe I hadn't thought of it before and connected the dots. It was one of the worst nights of my life — and it happened on New Year's Eve.

In November of my sophomore year in high school, I was asked on my first real date. Joe* was a popular boy and I'd had a crush on him for years. He was cute and funny and smart. We kissed in the backseat of his friend's mother's Wagoneer all the way home from a screening of *Grease*. It was my first kiss, and (to me) it was magic. Based on this one experience, I thought for certain we were meant to be together. I was so happy. But then weeks went by, and Joe didn't call.

Somehow that New Year's Eve I wrangled my way into a party given by an upperclassman. When I arrived, I saw Joe. To my relief, he was there with his best friend, Mike — not on a date. So as the clock ticked down towards midnight, I maneuvered my way through the crowded room to position myself strategically by my beloved. My plan was that at the moment when everyone shouted "Happy New Year!" I would be right beside Joe, awaiting his kiss.

My plan backfired. I guess I wasn't so stealth. Mike spied me mooning after his pal and took matters into his own hands. He walked up to me and said, "Listen, Joe doesn't feel **that** way about you."

My face grew hot and I couldn't breath. Mike seemed to be smirking. I turned and pushed my way through the crowd to get out of the house. I don't recall where I was at midnight, or if Joe even acknowledged my presence. Even today, decades later, I still wince with pangs of humiliation at the thought of that night.

What's more, I still loathed Mike. I carried the events of that night with me in more ways than one.

After being publicly humiliated at age 14 you might think that I would have learned my lesson about romanticizing a relationship, but no, quite the opposite. I just could not get it through my thick head that when a relationship ran its course, it was over. If I had been infatuated with the guy, I clung to the hope that someday he'd see the error of his ways, realize how incredibly awesome I was and beg me to date him again. Of course, this never happened, at least not the way I imagined it would.

A pattern formed. I only wanted what I could not have, and once I had the thing I thought I wanted, I no longer found it — or him — desirable. It became a form of addiction.

The truth was, I was in love with being in love. I didn't want a relationship. I just wanted to get high on the feeling of infatuation. I wanted the oh-my-God-I-can't-believe-he-likes-me-and-asked-me-to-the-prom dopamine rush.

I fell in love with guys, not for whom they really were, but for who I imagined they were or who they could be. Of course, if the guy did stick around long enough for me to get to know him, chances are I'd decide he wasn't right for some reason, and break things off.

If the guy just stopped calling, it was the worst possible scenario because then I'd ignore his rude behavior and make up more stories about how great he was and how wonderful my life would be when he finally came to his senses and realized he was desperately in love with me. I didn't notice how incredibly sick this pattern was until more than a year after my second divorce.

I was hooked on the roller coaster of emotions, the feeling of uncertainty. As long as he didn't call, I could fantasize about him. If he did call to ask me out, well, that was a rush too.

As 2011 rolled to a close, I nursed the familiar, dull throb of an unrequited-love hangover. For the past six month, I'd been involved in an on-again, off-again long-distance relationship. The circumstances were different, and (thankfully) the relationship ended with feelings of mutual appreciation and respect, but once again I had heard the words, "I just don't feel **that** way about you."

Although, intellectually, I knew our parting was truly for the best all the way around, the words stung as hotly as they had when I was fifteen years old. This year, rather than sink back into the old pattern of ignorance, attachment and aversion, I opened my eyes to look at reality. Instead of blaming someone else for my unhappiness, I took a deep look my own actions and ideas.

"Unless you listen to your suffering, unless you look deeply into your suffering, and embrace it tenderly with your energy of mindfulness, you cannot understand the roots of your suffering," Thich Nhat Hahn writes. "When you begin to understand the roots of your suffering, suddenly the energy of compassion, of understanding, arises. And understanding and compassion have the power to heal."[22]

As I thought about that awful New Year's Eve so long ago, I saw something I missed before. I realized my loathing was misplaced. All this time I thought of Mike as a dastardly villain who cruelly taunted me. What if I had it wrong? What if Mike wasn't an insensitive jerk who took pleasure in my misery and humiliation, like a wicked child who pulls the legs of spiders? What if he was really trying to spare me from making a fool of myself at that party? What if he had taken pity on me? What if that snide smirk was a look of anguished compassion for me?

Why did I assume that he meant me harm? He didn't even know me. I certainly didn't know him. Perhaps he saw that his friend Joe was being an ass by avoiding me rather than telling me the truth, and decided to help us both out? Why did I assume his intention was to ruin my life?

No matter how I sliced it, with my new insight I saw how Mike provided me with an important lesson. If I had been able to really hear him, I might have deduced that longing after someone who does not want to be in a relationship — no matter the reason — will only make me sick and deluded. Being disappointed that someone you like romantically doesn't like you back, is normal. Clinging to the idea of a person after he has made his feelings (or lack thereof) known is neurotic.

As the minutes ticked down December 31, 2011, the reality of my past patterns with relationships sunk in. I heard Mike's words for the first time with clarity: "Your life will be happier and more fulfilled when you accept reality."

How is it that I could have spent more than 30 years nursing a resentment of someone who may not have really intended me any harm? Maybe Mike was really a cruel bastard, but I suspect that's not the case at all. At worst, he was indifferent to my feelings, which doesn't quite qualify him as Satan.

The true source of suffering was within myself. I had fabricated a relationship based on one date that was (for me) spectacular, but mediocre for Joe. I rejected the reality that sometimes teenage boys are fickle and don't really want to date someone steady, or don't know how to have a relationship, or don't understand how much importance some girls place on a first kiss.

More than 30 years later, alone in my house on that New Year's evening, I let go of my resentment of Mike. My perspective shifted and the story I told myself about him changed.

(For the record, Mike, I'm sorry that I've loathed you all this time. I take back all the awful things I thought about you. I was young and immature and blind to reality. Thank you for trying to show me how crazy I was behaving, mooning after a boy who quite obviously didn't share my fantasy romance.)

Yes, letting go of my long-held resentment of that boy — who has since grown into a balding, potbellied, middle-aged man — was easy. Forgiving myself for enacting a pattern of behavior has been a bit more difficult ... but I'm getting there.

* The names have been changed to protect the guilty and innocent.

Chapter 10: Healing

Away Camp

The year Jack turned 12 he asked to go to a summer camp in Florida run by an evangelical Christian youth organization. I didn't know much about the organization itself, except that it had been around since before I was in junior high school. Back then, I attended some of their parties and functions and the group seemed rather benign. Some of Jack's friends had become involved with the group and, although he hadn't attended any of their other functions, he begged to go to the camp.

Until that year he showed no interest in going away to an overnight camp, but now he seemed ready. Granted, most nights he still slept with his beloved, threadbare Panda Ping and called for bedtime stories, but he was also walking home from school alone, riding his bike to the nearby park and navigating middle school mostly on his own. Of course, my instinct was to shelter him from experiences beyond my purview, but the camp looked fun and it seemed a safe way for him to exert some independence.

I had to let go. This is the nature of maturation: Children want freedom. All through his childhood I felt the push and pull — wanting to hold Jack tight and keep him safe, while knowing he must venture from my grasp so he can become strong and independent. It's a crazy-making parental paradox.

When Jack was a toddler, his father and I took him to the community pool. Even though a virtual horde of babies splashed happily in the six-inch-deep water of the shallow end, Jack timidly approached the wet stuff. He fretted over the water until he cautiously waded in, but he refused to submerge his face. He wouldn't even jump from the side of the pool into my waiting arms for fear of plunging beyond my grasp.

I was grateful he wasn't like some young children who I'd see running away from their mommas to leap precariously into deep water, but as he grew older, I felt frustrated by Jack's timid behavior. Why? I've never been a strong swimmer. I was terrified of the water as a kid and although I swim well enough to enjoy the beach or pool, I remember how limited I was at swim parties. When other kids were happily playing Marco Polo, I was the fish out of water. I wanted something better for Jack.

As much as his dad and I wanted him to learn how to swim, we didn't want him to have a bad experience in the water. So we waited until we felt he was up for the challenge.

At age four, we enrolled him in swimming lessons. He needed some encouragement, but he was ready. Within a few sessions, the instructor had Jack placing his face in the water and blowing bubbles. Soon he was dog paddling around the pool.

I had to let go of my fears of him drowning and allow him to go and do what was healthy for him to do. Not only did he learn to swim, but also became a member of the swim team, and (more important) today he's a very confident swimmer who loves the water. Summer camp was the next plunge.

The night before Jack left for camp, he was understandably excited and nervous. He stood on the edge of the unknown and hesitated. As we packed up his bug repellent and sunscreen, he expressed second thoughts about going. As in the past, I became frustrated. We had been planning this trip for six months! He had been so excited about going just days before.

My first instinct was to be dismissive of his fears and say something snappy like, "Oh you'll get over it once you're there." Fortunately, I was ready to set aside my opinions and really listen what he had to say. Perhaps for the first time, I heard and appreciated my son's fears.

"I've never done this before," he said.

Jack's candor was beautiful. It is so difficult for me to admit that I'm unsure of something and yet he was so open and honest about his fears. My perspective softened.

How often have I closed my eyes, gritted my teeth and blustered my way through life, denying all the while that I'm scared? Do I feel anxious when I travel to an unfamiliar city? Sure. Am I insecure when I get up to speak in front of a group of people I don't know? Heck yeah. Aren't I nervous when I'm pitching a new editor? Absolutely. And that anxiety, like any emotion, can be debilitating or it can be used as a source of information about myself.

I listened to Jack — really listened. He wanted to go to camp, but he was scared. It occurred to me that he felt the push and pull of growing up, too. He wanted to let go, to have a new experience and test his comfort zone, but he also wanted to remain a little kid, and to stay in the familiar where it was safe. Maybe his friends who were also going to camp didn't feel scared, so maybe he felt there was something defective in him for being anxious.

When I spoke, I told Jack how I get scared too and that it's normal to feel hesitant when you're doing something new and going somewhere you've never been before.

"Feeling anxious is not a bad thing," I said. "If you didn't feel a little anxious, I'd worry about you. We wouldn't have encouraged you to go to camp if we didn't think you were ready. You **are** ready for this."

Jack nodded as I outlined the evidence I saw that he was ready to go away to camp. I reminded him how he exercises good judgment, and how he's able to make friends so easily. I recounted how he did a great job in sixth grade handling all its new experiences and challenges. (And how he could survive on peanut butter and crackers when there were no chicken nuggets in the offing.) As I spoke, I knew in my heart my words were true. He was entirely ready to cross this emotional milestone. Maybe — just maybe — I was ready, too.

I turned out the lights. We had to get up at 4 a.m. to meet the bus that would carry him and his friends down to the campsite in Florida. He begged me to tell him stories until I was too sleepy to make sense.

I must have dosed off, but at midnight, Jack was still awake. He asked me to tell him another story. This time he requested a tale about a time I went away to camp.

Although my experiences were somewhat limited, I did attend a Girl Scout camp when I was in fifth grade. I thought for a moment about how it felt to sleep in a cabin away from home for the first time. Had I been homesick? Yes, I had. I remembered feeling alone and lost, but then another memory surfaced. It was one I had not recalled in a while.

One of the items I took to camp was a three-inch statue of the boy Jesus. The statue was made of a pale white plastic and it glowed in the dark. (It was the same little statue I carried with me on my infamous attempt to run away from home.) I also took a small plastic statue of Mary, Jesus' mother. I remember my friends and I playing with the statues at night in the same way we might have played with Barbie dolls. We made up conversations between Boy Jesus and Mother Mary. We were terribly irreverent, but we forgot the little ache of longing for our own beds and giggled ourselves to sleep.

"Hard to believe that your Buddhist mother took Jesus to camp," I said to Jack as I concluded the tale. Jack nodded. He was quiet for just a moment and then he piped up.

"You were an atheist for a while though, right?" Jack asked.

I thought for a moment.

"No, I don't think I was ever an atheist," I said. "I always believed there was something. I just didn't know what I believed. That's what you call an agnostic."

"I'm agnostic," said Jack.

"That's a good thing to be," I said. "It just means you're not sure what you know."

"I'm probably always going to be an agnostic," said Jack.

"That's fine," I said. "I'm an omnitheist now. That means I believe the divine is in everything."

Either Jack was finally exhausted or he was bored of the deepening conversation. He grew quiet and I soon heard his soft, even breathe.

As I drifted off, I marveled at the transformation that occurred within my life and within my family. I was providing my child what I had not been given: the opportunity to admit that he doesn't know what or who God is without fear of being ostracized. In that moment, my history shifted and generations of karma took a healthy turn. Our future story was rewritten.

At four a.m., as we drove across town in the dark to meet an enormous double-decker bus that would carry him away, Jack piped up from the back seat.

"I'm really excited and a little nervous and ... what's that A-word?" he asked.

"Anxious?" I said.

"Yes, anxious," he said, confidently.

Yes, he was ready.

When his friends arrived, Jack hugged me good-bye. Then he clambered into the to upper deck of the bus with his buddies where they could see the road roll out before them and glimpse what the future held.

Salvation

Jack was saved. Despite his firm commitment to agnosticism when he left for camp, my dear son was swayed to the Jesus-side by a 70' pool slide, a bungee jump called the Flying Squirrel and five nights at a fabulous Christian camp in Florida. Having only recently come to terms with my former Christian self, it was unsettling to think that my 12-year-old son might be in thrall to some of the same fear-mongering tactics that left me feeling spiritually inadequate for so long. But there was a difference: Jack was not me.

"I've decided I'm a Christian," Jack announced as he looked up from a YouTube video to gauge my reaction.

"Really?" I said, trying to hide my fear. "Wow! What does that mean?"

"That I believe Jesus was sent to earth by God to die for our sins," he said.

"What did we do that was so bad to warrant that?" I asked.

"Well, I guess for what Adam and Eve did, you know, the Original Sin," he responded and then went back to watching YouTube. "Why mom? Is there something wrong with that?"

"No," I said slowly, "but I am interested in hearing more about who you think God is."

As Jack told me that only people who believed in Jesus could go to heaven and enjoy eternal life, every fiber in my Roman Catholic Buddhist being wanted to scream, "No! There **is** something very wrong with that!" As Jack parroted (and paraphrased) Bible verses, I kicked myself for not taking a closer look at what that camp was all about.

I had spent more than 40 years finding my way to a loving, compassionate God. What I heard Jack say was that God only cared about a select few. That's not my idea of God. That's not the God who I've seen at work in the world. That is not the God who allows our planet to spin through space without crashing into the sun; the divinity that allows sperm and egg to create a new being; the God who provides peace to people who are suffering and lonely. That is not the Divine miracle that exists in every leaf, every cockroach, every blossom, every grain of sand in its perfection. It made me want to cry to think that Jack really believed God was anything less than unconditionally loving and compassionate.

Thankfully, a power greater than me kicked in. I held back my aversion to those fundamental beliefs. Maybe, just maybe, Jack translated what was imparted to him incorrectly. It's very possible that the well-meaning young camp counselors provided lessons that did not include threats of the pains of Hell, but it is more likely they did. I'd spent all my adult life shirking off discriminatory religious beliefs, finding compassion for those who are close-minded, and who monger hatred and discrimination. To have my dear son filling his cup with the very thing ... well, it was almost too much for me to bear. Almost.

Because the God of my understanding is kind and compassionate, and because I'm trying to walk on that kind and compassionate path, I engaged him in a discussion (hopefully) without making him feel defensive. At least that was my intention.

I encouraged him to think for himself, to challenge anything he was told to believe, to find his own truths. I told him that throughout history fear of Hell never led to loving action — only to more fear and hiding and deception and hatred and discrimination. Fear couldn't breed love any more than an apple seed can yield oranges, but with compassion, fear could be transformed into understanding.

We talked about what Jesus really said and — more important — what he did during his time on earth. We discussed how the *New Testament* was written long after Jesus' death by men who were not God and therefore could have possibly inserted their own ideals and viewpoints.

Instead of being afraid that my son had been "corrupted" by teenage evangelicals, I realized I should be thankful. Without this camp experience, I would not have had this conversation with Jack about God and Jesus and spirituality.

Was this Jack's way of rebelling against his dharma lovin' Momma? Probably not. Maybe this was spiritual evolution in action — for him and me.

Jack had never expressed much interest in spiritual matters. He resisted attending church; and although I took him to the Buddhist center for years, he was only in it for the treats dispensed before and after services. Was Jack's choice of Jesus over Buddha as a personal slap in the face? No.

Even though I wanted to defend the dharma over the gospels, I let it go. Let's face it, Jesus with his piercing blue eyes, hip, long flowing hair and sandaled feet has always been a sexier role model than the bald-headed, barefooted Buddha who, in his

Chinese restaurant effigies is often portrayed to be morbidly obese. (By the way, that's Hotei, a Chinese deity of abundance, not The Buddha.)

Maybe it's just the product of Western culture, but Jesus had better spin from the get-go. Not that I think spirituality is a beauty contest or a political campaign, because in the battle of Jesus versus Buddha there would be no contest. Literally. I mean, they just wouldn't fight. They would agree wholeheartedly.

And yet, talking with Jack about Jesus, I felt that age-old desire to defend my beliefs and to convince him that I was right and he was wrong. I felt the very thing that I would accuse the camp counselors of doing. I felt myself becoming rigid in my thinking and flushed with desperation to outline all the ways that Adam and Eve didn't exist and how there couldn't possibly be a harp quartet in heaven. I found myself falling into the same trap as the fundamentalists ... because at that point, I was one of them.

As hard as it was not to hit the alarm button and call forth a battalion of liberal-minded family members and friends to hold an intervention and undo Jack's brainwashing, I listened to my son.

As I questioned his statements, his responses were open and honest, and filled with love. He was so excited. He had an experience at that camp, and he embraced the idea that there might really be something greater than him. He might even want to develop his spiritual life some day. I realized this might be a significant milestone in Jack's life.

I believe we all have an entry onto our spiritual path. Within any given life time, there's a point where we can reach for knowledge of Good and Evil and — like Adam and Eve — we are cast out of our ignorance. I don't think we're dispelled from Paradise, but we're sent out onto the path of our own experience where we can learn what it means to have a spiritual nature. Perhaps Jack was now on his way.

And me? I'm on my way, too. I'm just at a different place on the path. I cannot walk Jack's path for him, nor can I keep him from taking detours or falling into ditches or stopping by the ice cream truck to get a popsicle. When I want to scream and warn him that fundamental thinking is a trap, I have to remember that I was right there where he was many years ago.

Once upon a time, I believed all the stories I was told about Jesus and the angels and saints and heaven and hell and purgatory. When I did begin to question, I thought there was something wrong with me. I thought that I would be disowned by my family if I didn't believe exactly as they did. I wasn't given an option or a chance to decide my spiritual beliefs for myself.

Ultimately, I did rebel, but not until after I had lied about my faith for decades. Yet, I started out just like Jack, loving Jesus and feeling so happy that God thought enough of me to send Jesus down to die for my sins. Here I am today — with a different set of beliefs — finally living my life as the person God made me to be.

Later that night, while Jack and I were playing Pokémon, I remembered I had an old wooden crucifix that had been my father's or maybe even my grandfather's. It hung on the wall of my Dad's apartment before he died. When we finished our game, I retrieved it from my dresser drawer and gave it to Jack. Before he went to bed, we placed the cross on his mantel next to the picture of his Grandpa Jack.

"Grandpa was a great Christian, wasn't he?" Jack said proudly.

"Yes, he was," I said, "and he lived by the teachings of Christ. He'd be very proud of you."

There are so many things I do not know, but those words were gospel truth.

As a parent, I want my child to benefit from what I've learned, and perhaps not make the same mistakes I've made. Why do I expect him to sidestep the difficulties that I had to slog through? I want Jack to have it easier, but maybe I've got it all wrong. What if he needs to go through the process of being swept away in an evangelical undertow to find acceptance? What if that's the path? What if it's necessary to follow before you can lead? Perhaps by trying to protect Jack from this experience, I'm depriving him of the opportunity he needs to define his own personal sense of spiritual practice and relationship with God? Maybe this is God's process. Maybe, just maybe, I should trust that process.

Whatever Jack decides to believe, my only hope for him is that he finds the peace and understanding that I have found. I have faith that he will — because that's what the God of my understanding wants for us all.

Chapter 11: Consciousness

Occupied China

Years before my mother was diagnosed with dementia she began divvying up her prized possessions and those items that held sentimental value. She told me that she wanted me to have her "good" wedding china. She recalled I had always admired those fancy dishes. I could not bring myself to tell her that I coveted her ornate china when I was a teenager. I didn't have the heart to point out that now that I was grown up, the pink flowers and gilding just weren't my style. When she first pressed the set upon me, I resisted.

"You may want to use them again," I said. "I'll get them next time."

Mom scrawled my name on a scrap of paper and placed it on top of the dishes. On subsequent visits, I made excuses for not taking the dishes. There was never enough room in my car; nor boxes large enough to hold the set; or enough time to pack them properly. My hesitance to take her gift went beyond our differing tastes in tableware. The idea that my mother was divesting herself of her most-cherished possessions was disturbing, and just a little too real. On a deeper level, I knew by accepting her cherished china I was accepting her imminent death. At that point in my life, I just wasn't ready.

I didn't know that she was succumbing to dementia, but perhaps she did. I didn't understand that by giving away her precious things, she might feel better about leaving this world behind. I politely refused to take her dishes until it became clear that my parents could no longer live alone in their home. When I finally did carry those gold-rimmed, fragile plates and saucers and cups from the home where I grew up, I knew my universe had shifted permanently.

For more than 50 years, those gold-rimmed china collected dust in my mother's hutch. They only saw the light of day on very special occasions, such as when a parish priest came to dinner. I would hazard a guess that the dishes were used no more than 100 times under the tenure of my mother's careful watch.

The complete set of china (12 formal place settings, plus serving pieces) was given to my parents as a wedding gift in 1951. Each dish was embellished with small violets and primroses about the lip. In the center of the plates there was a rose surrounded by a spray of smaller roses. Dusty pink was the most dominant color, and each piece was rimmed in gold. The name of the manufacturer, Moriyama China, was stamped on the back along with the words "Made in Occupied Japan."

Even as children, we knew the meaning of the words: Made in Occupied Japan. Our father served in the Pacific during WWII, and from in the womb we heard tales of battles on the islands of Saipan and Makin. The presence of the china in our household confirmed that the struggle for global domination had played out as if predestined. My Dad returned to the States in 1945, whole and sound, and six years later married my Mom and together they received the china as a nuptial gift.

For reasons I do not know, my mother chose not to use the Good China. She kept it protected and locked away perhaps out of sentimental attachment to a time when she was young and her life was full of possibilities. I will never know what that china represented to her. Was it a reminder of the finer things in life? Did she fear breaking or damaging a plate and therefore diminishing its worth?

I am hard pressed to recall the last time the Good China was used in our childhood home. As my parents inched into their late 80s, we did not have many grand meals around their maple dining table.

For four years the Good China took up residence in my own cupboards, unused. I already had a set of "good china" (also unused), but also I held fast the sentiment that Mom's dishes were precious and should only be used on *special occasions*. The delicate floral cups, saucers and plates gathered more dust, until I separated from my husband and moved into a little apartment of my own. I packed up all 90 pieces and brought them to my new home where they became my everyday china. Mom's dishes became symbolic of how I would live my life as I moved forward post-divorce.

All things change. I know this now all too well. In my desire to keep things "nice," my attachment to the shiny, golden, perfection in life led to my dissatisfaction. I might as well make the most of every moment and live in celebration rather than fear.

Today, my family consumes pizza, tacos and sandwiches from the gold-rimmed plate and eats Fruit Loops and ice cream from the bowls. The Good China is the only set of dishes we use. Yes, the flowers and gilding have faded from countless rounds in the dishwasher, but not one piece has been broken — so far.

Today, everyday is a special occasion. Everyday is precious. My mother placed my name on her 90-piece set of china, but the real gift she handed down to me was an appreciation for life.

The Nature of Things

It took almost a year of trial and error before I finally accomplished a feat central to Buddhist practice: meditation. Before my success, the word meditation was enough to make me squirm. It looked so easy, but for months I tried to meditate and failed miserably. I just could not sit down on a pillow and focus my mind for more than three minutes. The very thought of sitting for any length of time, doing nothing, thinking nothing conjured up a to-do list a mile long of tasks that I absolutely had to complete before I could meditate. So, I avoided sitting with my thoughts until I learned (as with so many things in life) I was going at it all wrong.

I always thought meditation required clearing one's mind of all thought. Of course, this is impossible. The mind perceives thought just as the eyes perceive sights and the ears perceive sounds. Therefore, expecting my mind not to entertain thought is as unrealistic as expecting my ears not to hear or my nose not to gather scent.

The idea of meditation is not to banish all thoughts, but to recognize the thought as a passing, temporary phenomenon — just like sound or light or an odor — and not get obsessed with it.

Meditation is central to Buddhist practice not because we are trying to levitate off the floor or drain our egos to nothingness, but because it allows us to practice a discipline of the mind. In other words, if I can learn to not be carried away by my thoughts of fear, anxiety or bliss when I'm sitting in meditation, it will be much easier to let go of distracting thoughts in my everyday life. Meditation becomes much like physical exercise. The more I workout, the more I build stamina and strength. In the same way, the more I meditate, the easier it becomes to sit for longer periods of time. After several years of practice, now (on most days) I look forward to sitting still for 30 minutes and simply observing my thoughts.

Recently, I sat down to meditate in my sunny, tranquil meditation room. I lit candles and incense and positioned myself comfortably on my meditation sofa. I set the timer for 30 minutes and corrected my posture. Focusing on the candle's flame, I began to concentrate on my breathing, placing light attention on the out-breath. I breathed in ... and out ... in and ... ugh. Every breath brought me closer to the reality ... that I was sitting in the proximity of cat pee.

The acrid aroma surrounded me. I stopped the timer, and sniffed the pillow next to me. My serenity abandoned ship. The unmistakable odor of cat urine permeated the cushion. I sniffed the bright Indian fabric that covered the sofa bench. It reeked. I pulled back the cloth and saw evidence of a stain on the large bench cushion. It was everywhere!

I quickly cast blame on the likely offender, our kitten Scarlett. She was nowhere to be found. If I caught her in the act, I might be able to correct her behavior, but now there was certainly no way to teach her a lesson about the appropriate use of her litter box. All I could do was strip the sofa of its slipcovers, remove the offending pillows and material, and treat it with bleach. My meditation time was ruined.

As I carried all the fouled material to the laundry closet, my thoughts turned to anger, blame and frustration. Why did we decide to adopt another cat? We already had one. If we had not taken in this stray, my meditation sofa would be fresh and clean right now. I should have known better! Some cats just can't be house trained. We already had one perfectly good cat. If that kitten does this again, she's going back to the pound! If I can't get this pee smell out I'll have to throw out the entire futon cushion and buy a new one! This is all my boyfriend's fault! He wanted another cat. I should have said no, but I wanted to please him. Me and my pleasing ways ... It's all my fault! I should have known better ...

On and on I seethed, piling up resentments, turning the anger and dissatisfaction over and over in my head. The irony wasn't lost on me. If ever there was a good time to practice compassion and forgiveness it was now. Instead of meditating, I spent the next 30 minutes fuming as I dowsed the slipcovers and cushions with diluted bleach.

In the following days I contemplated Scarlett's offense. At last, a new thought occurred to me. Scarlett was not a *bad* cat. She was simply carrying out cat behavior and instinct like the good cat that she was. In fact, Scarlett was a very *good* cat. The problem (for me) was that Scarlett was not a good human being. I could not reason with her or teach her to amend her behavior. I expected her to act in a manner that was not natural for her.

Scarlett did not pee on my meditation sofa out of revenge or spite or because she hated me or our other cat or Buddhism.

She peed on the cushion because she's a cat and she was marking her territory — which is what cats do. It's her nature.

How often do I expect people in my life to respond in ways that are not natural to them? Should I be angry with them, or more compassionate? Should I be more compassionate towards myself for holding onto unrealistic expectations? Einstein said the definition of insanity is doing the same thing over and over and expecting a different outcome. Expecting a different behavior from a being that is beyond his or her nature also leads to insanity. When I can see the reality of the situation, it makes it easier for me to let go of my attachment to what I want, and accept what is really happening.

As it turned out, my most dissatisfying meditation session taught me far more about compassion than sitting for hours in tranquility ever could. Simply contemplating that everyone wants happiness doesn't get me very far when I'm stuck in traffic or disputing a finance charge on my credit card with a less-than helpful customer service representative. No matter how long I sit on the meditation cushion and try to "generate compassion" for someone, I will never get far if I am still judging that person by my own limited viewpoint.

Chapter 12: Practice

Un-Stuck

For some strange reason I can see someone else's splinter-thin faults with 20-20 vision even when there's an enormous two-by-four protruding from my eye. Likewise, when things don't go my way, I am accustomed to finding a guilty party and promptly heaping on blame. I don't want to accept responsibility for my actions, so I am relieved when I can pin the guilt on someone — anyone — else.

When I first separated from my soon-to-be-ex, I blamed him for the demise of our marriage. If he had acted the way I wanted him to act, everything would have been fine. Even though I had done awful things to him and our relationship, I felt justified. My "Well, he started it!" mentality may have eased my burden, but only temporarily. Sooner or later I had to sit with the reality of the situation and own my part in the outcome.

When I seek someone or something to blame for a problem in my life, I am either trying to absolve myself of guilt, or I'm trying to justify the problem with a rationale. I so desperately need to understand why an outcome didn't go the way I wanted it to go that I fabricate a story to make myself feel better. "If the cat hadn't left her toy on the floor, I wouldn't have tripped and spilled my coffee! Now I have coffee all over my T-shirt and the floor and I'm going to be late for work ..." You get the idea.

Why do I need a reason to explain every event in life? Why can't I just be okay saying, "Shit happens," like bumper stickers prescribe? I need to find someone or something to blame so I can feel better. Blame relieves me from feeling that I screwed up, that I let other people down, or caused harm. If I can latch onto a cause, then maybe I can convince myself that I have no part in the effect.

Of course blaming others is just a temporary fix. After a while, the scapegoat approach will spring a leak and I'll have to admit that I'm powerless. Period. End of discussion. Blaming is part of my addiction to control because it's a way to deny reality. But mindfulness practice helped me get a handle on my compulsion to blame.

A few years ago, Jack and I travelled to Thich Nhat Hanh's Magnolia Grove Monastery for a family retreat. Hanh, of course, is a renowned Vietnamese Buddhist teacher, writer and peacenik. Magnolia Grove monastery is located in a remote area of Mississippi not far from Tupelo, the birthplace of another legendary incarnation, Elvis Presley.

That summer, we stayed at the Zen Buddhist retreat for four days in the middle of one of the hottest Julys on record. Jack, who was nine at the time, had been a real trooper navigating the Zen Buddhist traditions of mindful, communal living. For Jack eating in noble silence was an even bigger challenge since Magnolia Grove is strictly vegan and my son is strictly a chicken-nugget-avore. So as we packed up to leave that morning, I promised him we'd go from deep dharma to deep-fried and make Wendy's our first stop upon reentering the western world.

As much as I enjoyed our time at the meditation center, I admit I was relieved to conclude our stay. I looked forward to traveling on to my sister's comfortable, air-conditioned home in Little Rock for our annual Fourth of July activities.

I packed up the car before the heat of the day became unbearable and retrieved Jack from the playground where he was amusing himself. He piled into the backseat with his legion of stuffed animals, snacks and electronics. By 11 a.m. we were ready to hit the road.

Slowly, I edged out of the gravel driveway and turned to enter the country lane that runs in front of the monastery. But instead of easing onto the pavement, my car lunged downward. Too late, I realized my mistake: I had not cleared a four-foot ditch next to the drive. We stopped with an abrupt jolt. I heard the sickening crunch of fiberglass. My front fender, complete with "Loving Kindness is My Religion" sticker, was planted in terra firma. The rear spoiler tilted up to the heavens. There was no going forward. There was no backing out. I was stuck. I reacted in the manner one might expect of a new Buddhist practitioner.

"Oh shit!" I muttered.

"Mom, you cussed!" Jack said. "You owe me a quarter."

Jack and I were unhurt, but the car was wedged at an awkward angle, making the passenger door impossible to open. Jack had to scramble over the console and out the driver's side to safety. We stared at the car for a moment in quiet disbelief.

"Wow, Mom," he said, "you really wrecked the car!"

"I didn't wreck it ...," I said slowly. "The car just ... went ... into the ditch."

I crouched down to examine the nose of the car. The driver's side looked hideously crunched. The sound of cartoon cash register bells sounded off in my head. Cha-ching!

For a moment, a familiar feeling welled up inside of me. I wanted to blame this mishap on something or somebody — even myself or Jack. "We shouldn't have left the retreat early!" "We should have stayed for lunch." "If only Jack weren't such a picky eater, we wouldn't have been in such a hurry to get on the road." "Why do these stupid monastics have a ditch beside the road anyway? They should have posted a big warning sign."

Thankfully, after three days of rising at 6 a.m. to chant and pray, eating in noble silence, walking in contemplative meditation, listening intently to dharma talks and experiencing the sublimeness of guided meditation sessions, I couldn't muster the energy to dwell on my usual litany of "if onlys."

I had not been distracted by worrisome thoughts or the desire hurry to our next destination. One minute, Jack and I were turning out of the driveway; the next, we were stuck. I had miscalculated the turn. It was an accident. Since it was an auto accident, the thing to do was to call a tow truck to pull us out of the ditch. I hoped the car had not sustained serious damage, but it wouldn't help matters to worry about that now. If need be, I would have the car towed to the nearby town and wait for it to be repaired. I explained my plan to Jack.

"But Mom," he said. "What if we're stuck here forever?"

I could think of much worse fates than being stuck at Magnolia Grove for eternity. The tranquility and simplicity of this remote haven held hypnotic appeal. I understood why young nuns and monks were drawn to a lifestyle where happiness is the chief objective. But for a nine-year-old boy to be stranded without Wi-Fi, Internet access or cable was a fate worse than death. I assured him we'd be on our way soon, and suggested he go to the shady playground while I waited for the tow truck.

As Jack ran off to the play area, I looked at my car again and laughed. Perhaps it was the heat, or the contact-high of being around 30 monks and nuns who practice mindfulness 24-7, or maybe because I felt too embarrassed to throw a hissy fit about my wrecked car at a Buddhist monastery. No matter the reason, what I experienced that morning was nothing short of grace.

Perhaps for the first time in my life, I felt the desire to blame, but I didn't react to it. I felt the familiar compulsion to rationalize, but for some wonderful reason, I chose to let the feeling pass. Instead, I realized it wouldn't be helpful to get upset. Letting go of my habitual responses to an unexpected setback was a powerful feeling, so powerful that I was conscious of what was happening as it was happening. My car was stuck, but I was not.

Birds of the Air

We all want purpose in our lives — that elusive thing that makes us feel as though life has meaning. More than that, I want to know that my actions will be remembered.

When most people say, "What's my purpose in life?" What they mean is, "Who will remember me for all time?" This is egotistic, of course. Very few human beings are remembered for all time. When you think of all the billions of people who have walked this earth, very, very few of them are even mentioned in a history book. Only a few contributed in such as way as to earn some merit worthy of noting.

We live in a time when anyone — and everyone — can record their every action on Facebook, LinkedIn, Twitter and Instagram. We can literally leave our mark on the world everyday, because posts to these social media sites deposit their indelible digital fingerprints on the Internet, like the imprints of karma on mindstream. But does that mean the more than 1.7 billion people on Facebook will be remembered more than the people who lived and died in Pompeii? I don't think so.

It is impossible to live without leaving a mark on this earth. Every life yields a lot of actions that are taken for the benefit (or detriment) of that life. Sometimes we are aware of the marks we will leave behind and other times, we are not. But every action

The Nature of Things

leaves its effect. Often I will never know the lasting outcome my action will have. That's why I try to act with mindful intention, but sometimes that's hard to do.

Recently, while visiting friends the lake, we discovered a nest built by a dutiful mother bird on the dock. The tangle of grass and sticks sat on top of the receiver in a locked cabinet that held the stereo system. The eggs had hatched and four noisy chicks were trapped inside the cabinet.

With great care, my friends gently removed the nest with the chicks inside and placed them in a cardboard box on the dock. We were told (by someone who rescues wild critters and nurses them to health) that the mother would come for them. Although we all doubted the ability or the probability of a mother bird to swoop down and carry off her young, we had hope that this might happen; and yet, on that first night, there was no sign of momma.

My friend fed the chicks leftover grilled hamburger, and we tried not to think about their fate. Already these little birds touched our lives.

Saturday passed, and there was no sign of the mother bird. We were all saddened by the sound of the baby birds' cries. Again, my friend poked hamburger into the gaping mouths of the hungry babies. Only two were still alive. I wondered if the effort was futile, but I loved my friend for trying. After she fed the chicks, they quieted down for the night, stomachs full. My friend worried that she did not have a dropper to give them water. Would they die of dehydration?

God — in the form of Nature — provided what we could not. Sunday arrived with thunder and rain showers. We watched movies inside my friend's snug house and played cards on the covered porch. The cardboard box that held the fledglings grew damp, but the chicks' thirst was quenched.

By mid-afternoon the clouds began to clear and the sun came out. The children went outside to play and everyone followed. As my friend and I sat on the dock and talked, we heard a commotion coming from the box on the far edge of dock. I turned my head in time to see the shadow of a bird dip down into the box and then fly away.

"She's doing it!" we cheered. "The mother is feeding them!"

The mother bird returned with her beak filled with wriggling dinner for her surviving children. Their fate was still not certain, but the babies *were* being cared for, this we knew — and it was a relief for many reasons.

In this world, we want to know that mommas will return to care for their young and that the weak will survive. We want to see signs of compassion in the natural order of life. If we do not see these signs in nature, what hope can we have for ourselves?

No matter how hard I try, the rug will get pulled out from under me. I'm going to get sick. I'm going to get old. I'm going to die. That's the ultimate rug removal, right? That's how life **is**. That's the nature of all of life, not just mine. Life means change. Change means lack of control. As long as life changes, I will not be in control. Therefore I will feel powerless as long as life changes. Guess what? That's inevitable. But understanding that there is uncontrollable change happening all the time makes me a little anxious. What's a girl to do?

Watching these birds, reminded me of that verse from *Matthew* in the *New Testament* entitled, *The Cure for Anxiety*.

"For this reason I say to you, do not be worried about your life, as to what you will eat or what you will drink; nor for your body, as to what you will put on. Is not life more than food, and the body more than clothing? Look at the birds of the air, that they do not sow, nor reap nor gather into barns, and yet your heavenly Father feeds them ... So do not worry about tomorrow; for tomorrow will care for itself. Each day has enough trouble of its own."[23]

In so many ways, I am like that mother bird who does her best, but sometimes miscalculates the outcome. I cannot know with certainty if I'm providing security for my child or putting him in harm's way. Yet, I would be unable to walk through life if I did not have some type of understanding — if not faith — that there was a power greater than me at work in the world. Sometimes this power is simply Mother Nature and the divine order of the world.

This trust is important because I can see that my exact nature is part of the natural world. Like all of nature, I respond in a way that is informed by my experience and environment. I make the best decisions I can at the time, and then let go of the outcome. Like the momma bird, I make my decisions based on the information at hand. A locked stereo cabinet *was* the safest place to build a nest. She did not take into account that human beings would return to the dock and open the cabinet and want to play John Prine. Her wise choice turned fatal for her chicks when the circumstances beyond her control changed.

Like the momma bird, I can only do my best with the information I have — and give myself a break for not being omniscient. The knowledge I possess now is greater than the knowledge I had four minutes ago, let alone four years ago. I am still responsible for my past actions, but I cannot live my life in fear of what might come next.

It is more important to move forward with reverence, understanding and compassion, knowing that every life touches and influences every other life in some way, great or subtle. And every great or subtle nudge gently prompts us to look up or down or see things we haven't seen before, or shut down and refuse to speak at all. My response is my choice — and my legacy. Nothing is wasted. No person is insignificant. No life is incidental. Every action matters.

The Nature of Things

Brigid Elsken Galloway

The Nature of Things

About the Author

Brigid Galloway practices Buddhism and a 12-step approach to life in Birmingham, Alabama. She is a faculty member of The Institute for Conscious Being where she teaches the spirituality of the Enneagram and shares her meditative approach to writing as a means for spiritual discernment.

Galloway is a freelance writer, editor and journalist. As such, she reported for **NPR**'s *All Things Considered*, *Marketplace* and local public radio affiliate **WBHM**. Her feature stories have been published in local and national specialty publications and on websites, including *Tiny Buddha*. She was previously a deputy editor in Time Inc.'s custom publishing division and director of advertising for Turner Network Television.

Galloway writes about her spiritual journey in her blog, *Adventures of a Southern Buddhist Catholic*.

Reference Notes

[1] Chodron, Pema. *When Things Fall Apart.* (Massachusetts: Shambhala Publications, Inc., 1997)

[2] Ibid

[3] Lao-tzu. *Tao de Ching* translated by Stephen Mitchell. (New York: Harper Perennial Modern Classics, 2006), Section 33.

[4] Williams, Margery. *The Velveteen Rabbit:* (New York: Doubleday, reissued, 1991)

[5] Hanh, Thich Nhat. *For a Future to Be Possible*: *Commentaries on the Five Mindfulness Trainings.* (California: Parallax Press, 1993)

[6] Chodron, Thubten. *Buddhism for Beginners.* (New York: Snow Lion Publications, 2001)

[7] Chodron, Thubten. *Buddhism for Beginners.* (New York: Snow Lion Publications, 2001)

[8] Pascal, Blaise. *Pensées.*(1670)

[9] Hanh, Thich Nhat. *You Are Here.* (Massachusetts: Shambhala Publications, Inc., 2001)

[10] Shantideva. *The Way of the Bodhisattva* translated by Pakmakara Translation Group. (Massachusetts: Shambhala Publications, Inc., 2006)

[11] Mitchell, Stephen. *The Gospel According to Jesus.* (New York: Harper Perennial Modern Classics, 1991)

[12] Tolle, Eckhart. *The Power of Now.* (California: New World Library and Canada: Namaste Publishing, 1999)

[13] Hanson, Rick, *Hardwiring Happiness.* (New York: Harmony Books, 2013)

[14] Vilfredo Pareto's 80/20 Rule: from Wikipedia.org

Reference Notes

[15] Emerson, Ralph Waldo. *from "Experience," Essays: Second Series Essays, 1884.*

[16] Milarepa *A Song on the Six Perfections* translated by Ken McLeod. unfetteredmind.org

[17] Hanh, Thich Nhat. *You Are Here.* (Massachusetts: Shambhala Publications, Inc., 2001)

[18] Jung, Carl. *The Structures and Dynamics of the Psyche,* Collected Works of Carl Jung, Volume 8. (New Jersey: Princeton University Press)

[19] Hanh, Thich Nhat. *Buddha Mind, Buddha Body.* (California: Parallax Press, 2007)

[20] Chodron, Pema. *When Things Fall Apart.* (Massachusetts: Shambhala Publications, Inc., 1997)

[21] Nye, Naomi Shihab. *Never in a Hurry.* (South Carolina: University of South Carolina Press, 1996)

[22] Hanh, Thich Nhat. *Make a True Home of Your Love.* Dharma Talk from Plum Village, December 26, 2010, reprinted in The Mindfulness Bell, Issue 57. Summer, 2011.

[23] Matthew 6:25-34, *New American Standard Bible.* (California: The Lockman Foundation, 1995)

Made in the USA
San Bernardino, CA
27 September 2016